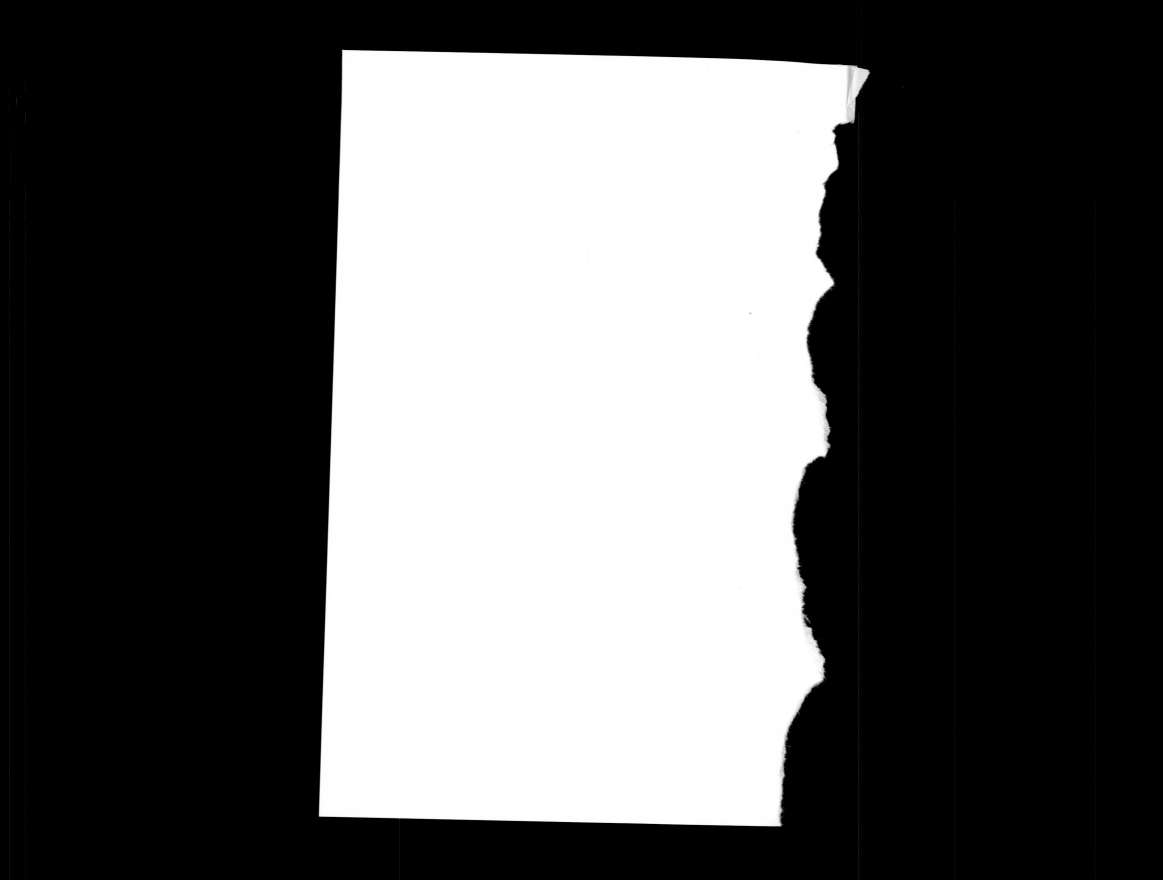

FIGHTING
the FLEET

TITLES IN THE SERIES

FIGHTING *the* FLEET

OPERATIONAL ART AND MODERN FLEET COMBAT

JEFFREY R. CARES AND ANTHONY COWDEN
FOREWORD BY ADM SCOTT SWIFT, USN (RET.)

NAVAL INSTITUTE PRESS
ANNAPOLIS, MARYLAND

Naval Institute Press
291 Wood Road
Annapolis, MD 21402

Library of Congress Cataloging-in-Publication Data
Names: Cares, Jeffrey R., author. | Cowden, Anthony, date, author. |
    Swift, Scott H., writer of foreword
Title: Fighting the fleet: operational art and modern fleet combat /
    Jeffrey R. Cares, and Anthony Cowden ; foreword by ADM Scott
    Swift, USN (Ret.)
Other titles: Operational art and modern fleet combat
Description: Annapolis, Maryland : Naval Institute Press, [2021] |
    Series: Blue & gold professional library | Includes bibliographical
    references and index.
Identifiers: LCCN 2021031243 (print) | LCCN 2021031244 (ebook) |
    ISBN 9781682477274 (hardcover) | ISBN 9781682477342 (epub) |
    ISBN 9781682477342 (pdf)
Subjects: LCSH: Sea-power—United States—History—21st century. |
    Military doctrine—United States—History—21st century. | Naval
    tactics—History—21st century. | Naval art and science. | United States.
    Navy. | Operational art (Military science)
Classification: LCC VA58.4 .C37 2021 (print) | LCC VA58.4 (ebook) |
    DDC 359.40973—dc23
LC record available at https://lccn.loc.gov/2021031243
LC ebook record available at https://lccn.loc.gov/2021031244

29 28 27 26 25 24 23 22   9 8 7 6 5 4 3 2

CONTENTS

CONTENTS

ILLUSTRATIONS

FIGURES

TABLES

FOREWORD

After a forty-year career in the Navy from enlistment to retirement, followed by just over two years of retirement, I have found myself committed to encouraging those still serving in the naval service to think more deeply about the profession of naval arms. Some of my perspectives are extensions of my experience in uniform; some are new, reshaped by my experiences since retiring. All caused me to jump at the offer to write the foreword for Jeff and Tony's consequential book for a consequential time.

Since retiring I have continued to remain engaged in a broad range of interests, principally in the development and application of military power, national power interests, and their application in an increasingly complex international environment. The world today is one where the consistency of the norms, standards, rules, and laws that have governed international economic, business, and trade relationships since the end of World War II has been significantly altered. Perhaps the most significant and compelling development from a national security perspective in the last ten years is the emergence of China as a peer competitor, especially in the maritime domain. This is certainly true from a force generation, capability, and capacity perspective. Right behind China is Russia, but as more of a "spoiler" than a true peer competitor.

China competes with the United States in every domain of national power. They do so with a grand strategy that is fully integrated nationally and internationally, through all elements of Chinese governmental power.

Whether measured and assessed ministry by ministry, domain by domain, or country by country, one can't help but pause and marvel at the arc of success the Chinese Communist Party has enjoyed over the last ten years. From this perspective it may be easier to understand, if not accept, my characterization of Russia as a spoiler.

Russia simply does not have the combination of national power elements—diplomatic, informational, military, or economic—in the same league as China. This is not to say Russia's national power and its ability to impose its national will in the sovereign space of other countries are things we can afford to ignore. Nations that lack the national power of their competitors often pursue asymmetric ways to employ what national power they do possess. Russia's demonstrated ability to apply its national strength in innovative ways demands serious consideration. An example of this is the Russo-Ukrainian conflict, with the employment of Russian soldiers wearing uniforms without national or unit insignias. Only a few years prior, in the Russo-Georgian conflict, "information warfare" was used to shape the opening, execution, and closing of that conflict. The Russian strategy in Syria has followed a similar formula of taking advantage of local opportunities to pursue strategic national objectives, avoiding the superior power of competitors while exploiting their vulnerabilities. These are just a few examples of successful application of innovative tactics to achieve strategic state objectives, despite Russia's relatively limited capabilities and capacity for peer competition.

I share these examples of the juxtaposition of the national power of China and Russia to provide context for the value of the book Jeff and Tony have written. This backdrop for the strategic value of the book is critical, as the book probes operational level of war considerations to ensure tactical actions achieve their intended function. These operational considerations are fully informed with respect to the science of applying kinetic effects as well as the more subjective elements of the art of war, such as variabilities of weather, logistics, system functionality, readiness, training quality and quantity, and human decision making, just to name a few. This book provides instruction and guidance on how to apply rigor to what is too often relegated to the realm of intuition. The goal is to provide understanding and fill knowledge gaps when facing the actions of peer competitors in fleet actions.

I have been fortunate throughout my career to be associated with individuals who were much smarter than I and to have the humility to recognize the critical opportunity to learn from them. This is what Jeff and Tony have provided in this book. They have applied the wisdom of such great tactical practitioners and operational thinkers as Rear Adm. J. C. Wylie and Rear Adm. Bradley Fiske and, more recently, Capt. Wayne P. Hughes Jr. Their book is the result of studying the works of such operational planners, analysts, and experts and applying their learning to modern fleet combat.

This book is at times not an easy read. It is a textbook that will challenge you to think, a book to be read in detail while making extensive highlights and notes in the margins—notes of alignment with the authors' experience and beliefs but also notes where one's views might diverge from the authors' views. I am hopeful that these concepts will be discussed in a Socratic environment, inclusively with subordinates, peers, and seniors and then applied in wargames, exercises, modeling, and simulation, creating a rich environment for review, assessment, and applied learning.

Given the environment of peer and near-peer competition we now live in, we cannot afford to treat conflict and war itself as a schoolhouse. The velocity of war our peers will achieve makes a "learn-as-you-go" philosophy incapable of overcoming strategic deficits. On today's battlefields every test will be a final exam graded not on a bell curve of learning but on a flat line of pass/fail. Today's warriors in competition and conflict, especially in the maritime domain, must arrive at the point of contact ready to teach an adversary by successful application of operational art, or risk suffering strategic failure.

As explained in the text, this book focuses on the intellectual space of the operational art of war. Operational art, and the operational level of war itself, is not the natural domain of naval officers, most of whom cut their teeth as tactical operators. As an aviator, my abilities were greatest within the confines of the cockpit and expanded by the range of my sensors. This was a world that was formed on the "science" of warfare, and it provided me with a weapons system that I became proficient in employing to achieve tactical effects. As I became more experienced and senior, my system expanded to include that of a wingman, then a division, and, with time and experience, as a strike leader. The common thread that connected all these certifications was a level of expertise and proficiency in the tactical application of the science of warfare.

Even after completing the Command and Staff curriculum at the Naval War College, serving as a squadron commander and, eventually, an air wing commander, my area of expertise was bounded by the tactical domain of war. It was also the metric against which my value to the Navy was assessed. It wasn't until I was assigned as a strike group commander and had the opportunity to participate in the Navy's Global 9 wargame that I was first exposed to the operational level of war as a practitioner. I summed my main takeaway from this experience as the necessity for the Navy to expose its commanders, train its captains, and test its flag officers in command on the operational level of war. It is in these three ranks that the application of Naval warfare begins the transition from the science of warfare to include the art of warfare.

The science of warfare is largely objective and binary, consisting of objective assessments of right/wrong, yes/no, black/white, day/night, one/zero. The art of warfare is much more subjective, neither right nor wrong, black nor white. It is a subjective, gray world defined by risk and uncertainty—risk both known and unknown. It is a world difficult to fully understand and harder still to quantify, one we are not comfortable in, and one we have had inadequate tools to evaluate. Jeff and Tony provide the tools and considerations that, when appropriately applied, increase order in what appears to be a disorganized battle space. By reducing the gray space of uncertainty, we reduce the leverage our adversaries have to exploit our weaknesses and mitigate our strengths.

There is a lot of science in this book. That is not to say this book is focused on the tactical level of war. In reading it, I found it just as critically informative and valuable in thinking about strategic objectives and opportunities as at the operational and tactical level of war. If those who operate at the tactical level of war don't have an appreciation of the operational effects their tactical actions are designed to achieve, the probability of sustaining the velocity of war (speed applied in the pursuit of objective) needed for success is much reduced. Likewise, if those operating at the operational and strategic level of war do not understand or recall the implications of constraints (must do) and restraints (cannot do) at the tactical level, no amount of art or subjective thinking will overcome the inability to achieve meaningful tactical effects in support of the operational plan and strategic vision. Retaining the understanding contained within this text is critically important to success at the operational and strategic level of war, as this book provides the foundation necessary to retain parity with our most consequential competitors. It provides us the tools we must embrace to leverage risk as a critical resource in achieving success in competition and victory in conflict.

Wisdom is not inherited with increased seniority. Those senior leaders we admire most, those who were tested in consequential ways in war while leading at the operational and strategic level, rose to greatness not with an inherent wisdom. Their wisdom was derived from experience and intellect informed by the retention of the rules of science that apply to the tactical and operational levels of war. They recognized the sum of tactical successes would never result in an equation of strategic success without the critical bridge between the two: operational art, applied in the development of an operational plan to guide the pursuit of combat operations. This book will help us get there.

In 1922 then-major George Patton was attending the field officer's course at the Cavalry School at Fort Riley. It was during this period that the following quote has been attributed to him: "Untutored courage is useless in the face of educated bullets." Depth of magazines, strength of extended supply lines, effectiveness of weapons systems, and efficiency of leadership are all increased and enhanced with "educated bullets." Reading, understanding, and teaching the key elements of this book will provide the "educated bullets" necessary to win a war with peers and near peers.

—ADM. SCOTT SWIFT, USN (RET.)

ACKNOWLEDGMENTS

The authors are indebted to a wide range of individuals who helped make this book possible. At the risk of leaving someone out, the authors would like to thank Tom Cutler of the Naval Institute Press, who was immensely supportive of this project; Adm. James Stavridis, USN (Ret.), whose support and encouragement were critical; Adm. Scott Swift, USN (Ret.), who generously contributed the foreword; and Rear Adm. Jeff Harley, USN (Ret.), for his support of the elective taught at the Naval War College that was based on the contents of this book. We would be remiss if we didn't acknowledge the officers and sailors of the flag and fleet staffs with whom we have served. Our shipmates' battle with the extremely challenging and complex problem of fleet planning was seen enough times and in enough circumstances to motivate this search for better answers for the fleet.

More personally, Capt. Wayne P. Hughes Jr., USN (Ret.), deserves our deepest thanks for decades of mentorship and for his direct and enthusiastic support of this book. Wayne loved Fiske's work and held Wylie in great esteem, and he led us to do so as well. He will be sorely missed. Of course, our long-suffering spouses, Betty Cares and Suzanne Cowden, cannot be thanked enough.

INTRODUCTION

Over the last half century, there have been two generally accepted approaches to the study of maritime strategy. The first has been an analysis of the component elements of maritime strength, [along the lines of Mahan]. The second approach, more prevalent in our generation, is the discussion of strategy in terms of specific types of operations such as fast carrier strikes, anti-submarine warfare, or organized overseas transport. I think both of these avenues of approach tend to obscure . . . the coherent form of the basic strategy that lies between these two, the strategy that grows from the components to give continuity and direction to the operations. It is this middle ground that I shall explore, the area in which a basic element of strength is transformed by an idea into a positive action. It is a sailor's concept of strategy, what it is, how it works, to what end it is followed, and what its problems are.

—REAR ADM. J. C. WYLIE, USN

One might be excused for thinking that this is a history book, describing how fleets operated throughout the ages. After all, it has been more than seventy years since the last great sea battles of World War II. Didn't the Cold War also end long ago? And hasn't the U.S. Navy enjoyed nearly thirty years of naval dominance—allowing it to become a power projection force par excellence with undisputed lines of communication to just about anywhere in the world? Isn't sea power now simply an enabler for warfare with joint forces, most valuable for providing strategic heavy lift, furtive reconnaissance, or long-range fires for a fight ashore?

The "Enabler-Navy" concept was the prevailing wisdom when this book was first envisioned. The first draft of this introduction, in fact, included a long argument to convince skeptics that perhaps the days of an American *Pax mari* were fading. But big changes can come quickly, even on strategic timelines: a view that the U.S. Navy must prepare for a high-end naval competition from more than one nation has become more widely accepted. One potential contender is a former foe, now resurgent, and the other is a continental power with a growing navy and extreme dependence on global commerce. Perhaps there will be another. The U.S. Navy is now looking to influence peer naval powers, to shift maritime risk to its adversaries, to control the terms of a long-term naval competition, and to be ready to engage at sea.

To achieve these ends will require more than just better naval strategy and policy, and more than just technological innovation. It will require a renaissance in an underappreciated and poorly understood subject, naval operational art. That's what this book is about.

WHERE IS OUR OPERATIONAL ART?

War colleges teach that there are three levels of war: tactical, operational, and strategic. The tactical level of war is fine-scale competition, where the actual fighting happens. The strategic level of war is coarse-scale competition, the place where such considerations as national goals, alliances, and theater-wide control are brought to bear. In between these levels is the operational level of war, which enjoys neither the concreteness of tactics nor the broad scope of strategy but instead brings together otherwise unconnected elements of both. At once part detail and part concept, planning at the operational level of war requires skill in what is called operational art, an ability to devise a pattern of tactical activities that support strategic goals. For many years and for various reasons, naval officers have not been very good at naval operational art.

Why is this so? Some may say that the historical role of the commander at sea—part sailor, part diplomat, part independent warrior—keeps naval thought at the extremes of the levels of war. Others may point to a modern navy's focus on success in technical "mission areas," such as antisubmarine warfare, which reward tactical proficiency and reinforce warfare community tribalism, breeding out cross-functional skillsets. Perhaps it is a preoccupation with technology and the tyranny of the acquisition process, where platforms and systems became ends instead of means. Any serving officer would have observed these behaviors enough to give credence to such claims. Moreover, two and a half decades of naval dominance can't have but dulled our appreciation for war at sea. A further cause, then, could be that almost all the naval leaders with peer-competitor naval experience at the operational level of war are in retirement.

A counterintuitive explanation would be the mandate for system-wide "jointness," ushered in by the Goldwater-Nichols Act of 1986, an edict designed to increase our understanding of operational art. The Navy was demonstrably late on board, so early joint doctrine was dominated by non-naval concepts and ground-centric ideas about warfare.[1] As a result, it can be fairly claimed that existing joint language is insufficient to describe the uniqueness of naval operations. Insofar as we can speak about operational art, it is the joint flavor we understand, not our own. And fleet officers speak fleet language—when they can't recognize that language in operational-level doctrine, operational art seems alien, sterile, and lifeless.

Whatever the reason, the fact remains that current operational level of war doctrine—the prevailing manifestation of naval operational art—won't explain how a fleet works. The main purpose of this book is to rectify this condition.

Operational art is one way to convey the past to the present. This book reaches into the rich and relevant language from our naval operational art heritage and recasts it for the modern reader. The benefits of this are manifold. If made valid and relevant to the modern sailor, naval operational art should capture and incorporate modern experience as all navies adapt to new challenges. Any sailor with fleet experience can have a voice in these discussions, but only after we establish a common language for emerging concepts, for incorporating the present into our naval future, and more importantly, for understanding historical precedents for what our potential adversaries might be planning.

Perhaps a shorthand definition of what naval operational art provides is that it describes what admirals do. True, flag officers and their staffs do preside over the operational level of war, but that doesn't imply proficiency. Rear Adm. Bradley Fiske captured this idea so succinctly in his 1905 U.S. Naval Institute prizewinning essay, "American Naval Policy," that it deserves to be quoted here in its entirety:

> Now there is no such word as "admiralship." There is such a word as "seamanship," and we hear it often in the Navy. There is also such a word as "generalship"; and no word in the English language conveys a nobler thought; no word expresses a higher idea of the power a single man can wield. Surely no thoughtful officer can feel that the admiral who will command our fleet in war will have less need for skill in fleet handling than a general has for skill in army handling, or that fleet handling is easier than army handling. And while one may feel that the essential qualities and principles of admiralship are the same as those of generalship, he will recognize the fact that the conditions of handling fleets are so different from the conditions of handling armies, that the science and art of admiralship must be developed as entirely distinct from generalship; just as distinct as they are from seamanship.[2]

A staff officer reading this book might get as far as the first few pages of the next chapter and exclaim, "An admiral will never read this . . . it's full of math and equations!" The same could be said of a technical text in introductory seamanship or airmanship skills, yet admirals and staff officers certainly must have mastered them at one time or another. Yes, the reader will indeed find mathematics in these pages, but there is nothing here more challenging than the math behind basic celestial navigation or aviation ground school. And while no one should argue that understanding the declination of stars or what the Reynolds number means to lift should be excluded from the education of a good deck officer or naval aviator, neither should one argue that these facts alone would make a top-notch sailor or pilot. That comes from years of experience in fleet operations.

We have the unhappy condition in our fleet that many officers serve on operational staffs and rise to flag rank without ever being exposed to, say, the impact of the salvo equations or search theory on the operational level of war. Thankfully, it has been many decades since this knowledge has been needed. Some self-taught students may have researched the subjects contained in this book along the way, but most have not. For those who have not, this book is also a remedial primer.

NAVAL OPERATIONAL ART HERITAGE

In our journals, naval professionals routinely write about what a navy does, but far less is being written about how a navy works. Perhaps this is because as naval officers we assume we all know innately and agree implicitly upon a description of the fundamental elements that make a navy, well, a navy. Maybe we expect that someone, somewhere must be researching and teaching such foundational concepts, say, at the Naval War College, the Naval Academy, or the Naval Postgraduate School. While this is a very old subject that was once studied intently by some of the Navy's most senior officers, it now holds at best a minor place in both the fleet and navy classrooms. Most contemporary writers of doctrine are too focused on function, organizational block diagrams, or lists of principles, not unlike cookbook authors more concerned with dictating proper kitchen procedure than with making the best meal.

There was a time, now long past, when fundamental questions about the art and science of naval operations were fervently discussed and debated in public. During what has been called the Golden Age of Tactical Thought (in a period following the shift from sail to steam, roughly from about 1880 until 1914), navies throughout the world struggled to comprehend the implications of a new era of large machines at sea. The pages of the U.S. Naval Institute *Proceedings* magazine, for example, were filled with articles—quite heavy on math and engineering—that proposed innovative tactical models and new ways to value the power of a fleet.

Perhaps the best culminating study of this period is Rear Adm. Bradley Fiske's *The Navy as a Fighting Machine*, written in 1916.[3] Fiske, Naval Academy Class of 1874, was one of the navy's first electrical engineers, playing a major role in developing most of the ship-control electromechanical devices that empowered big, rifled guns in battleships. He also had a full career at sea, including gunboat service at Manila Bay, soon after graduating from the Naval War College in 1896. A prolific writer, his prizewinning 1905 *Proceedings* essay "American Naval Policy" is still an insightful work on naval tactics, operational art, and fleet constitution and includes an early discussion on the challenges of what today we term anti-access/area denial tactics.[4] As a senior officer, he was a member of the General Board and served as the secretary of the Navy's aide for operations (a role much like today's chief of naval operations, or CNO). He was also president of the Naval Institute from 1911 to 1923, longer than anyone else. He lobbied so hard to create the CNO position that he found himself exiled to Newport in 1916, where he was given a room and a desk at the Naval War College— and time to think.

It was then that he wrote *The Navy as a Fighting Machine*, and although there are pockets of enthusiasm for his work, Fiske is barely known in modern naval circles. Fiske was an engineer, and he approached the topic with an engineer's sensibilities, describing the Navy for the first time as a whole of people, machinery, and doctrine. Noting that the U.S. Army was busy mechanizing as well, Fiske took care to show how a navy is quite different, and he explored how a modern navy fights. His description of the Navy as a machine still corresponds well to today's fleet, and there are many lessons for a modern reader. Perhaps his most profound observation was a warning not to expect "genius on demand" from our fleet leadership. In his view, naval warfare was becoming so complex that it demanded a deep intellectual commitment in peacetime because failure to do so would leave us wishing we were smarter when war came again.

Technology stabilized after World War I, and navies embraced newer technologies surrounding aircraft at sea. Senior naval officers at the Naval War College reduced the fundamentals from the Golden Age of Tactical Thought to practice in the interwar period. The planning and institutional genius developed in Newport between the wars served us well in World War II—so well, in fact, that it was some time before the senior ranks produced another important work on naval operational art. This time it was produced by another flag officer who was given a room, a desk, and time to think—Rear Adm. J. C. Wylie.

Wylie was commissioned from the Naval Academy in 1932 and saw significant combat as a mid-grade officer in World War II, receiving the

Silver Star for service at Guadalcanal. As one of the first officers with experience using radar in combat at sea, he was brought stateside to develop and codify shipboard Combat Information Center procedures before returning to the fight. He attended the Naval War College in 1949 and returned to serve on its staff from 1951 to 1953 and again, as chief of staff, in 1966. During his first staff tour he developed the Course of Advanced Study in Strategy and Sea Power. He served in sea billets typical of the time as well as in senior staffs (for example, as assistant chief of staff for operations at Atlantic Fleet headquarters and as deputy commander in chief, U.S. Naval Forces, Europe). Wylie was also a *Proceedings* contributor, and his 1957 essay "Why a Sailor Thinks Like a Sailor" resonates with many who question the ability of joint doctrine to capture naval thought.[5] This line of inquiry was expanded and meshed into an overarching theory of combat in *Military Strategy: A General Theory of Power Control* (1967).[6] Despite the title, a modern reader would recognize its content as operational art: "sequential" (ground) and "cumulative" (naval and air) patterns of warfare are described and compared in a comprehensive treatise on why services do their jobs so differently. Wylie concluded that control was the aim of all warfare, presaging John Boyd's "Patterns of Conflict" briefings.[7] He understood that determining what to control was the hard part of operational and campaign planning. In the quote at the head of this chapter, he is of course talking not about strategy as we think of it today but about naval operational art.

It wasn't until a generation later that another senior officer, Capt. Wayne P. Hughes Jr., made significant contributions to the theory of how navies fight. Hughes was commissioned at Annapolis in 1952, and after duty in minesweepers and destroyers in Korea and Vietnam, he became a pioneer in the relatively new field of naval operations research. He served as deputy director, Systems Analysis Division, in the Office of the CNO and as executive assistant to the undersecretary of the Navy before assuming the chair of Applied Systems Analysis at the Naval Postgraduate School, where he remained for many years as a professor of operations research and dean emeritus. Hughes is best known for his book *Fleet Tactics*, which first appeared in 1986.[8] In addition to *Fleet Tactics*, Hughes was a prodigious contributor to *Proceedings* and the *Naval War College Review*, providing thought-leadership on such topics as naval doctrine, maneuver warfare, strategy, and force structure. Hughes' most underappreciated work, however, was the development of salvo warfare theory, which describes the character of the transition from the age of gunnery, up through the dawn of carrier strikes to modern missile combat.

This book draws directly on the corpus of each of these researchers—Fiske, Wylie, and Hughes—and the reader would certainly profit by reading each of their major works independently. However, each wrote about more than just operational art, and the context in which their work emerged has changed a great deal since first publication. The intent of this book is to extract those parts of their work most relevant to today's challenges, update them for the modern reader, and combine them with other independent research conducted by the present authors.

ORGANIZATION OF THE BOOK

There are two main ideas in this book. The first is that fleets have four functions—striking, screening, scouting, and basing. The second is that operational art—admiralship, if you will—is a competitive scheme that brings these four together for victory. This is what Wylie meant by giving "continuity and direction" to naval operations.

The book has five primary chapters, along with this introduction and a conclusion. Chapter 1 discusses the sources of naval power and formally presents salvo theory, drawing heavily on Fiske and Hughes. Chapter 2 is concerned with surveillance and search, making the argument that these are the only two fundamental processes by which information is obtained from a battle space. Chapter 3 describes naval logistics, naval maneuver, and the importance of bases. It also presents an important difference between naval and ground-centric operational art: a naval operational reserve is force reconstituted from logistics, not force held in reserve. Chapter 4 brings the previous three chapters together into a coherent whole by presenting the four main functions of fleets—striking, screening, scouting, and basing—in the context of the classic competition between superior fleet and inferior fleets, arriving at a twenty-first-century definition of control consistent with Wylie's approach. Chapters 1 through 4 conclude with a set of implications and lessons for fleet planners and flag officers. Chapter 5 is a study of how the concepts from this book might inform operations with future platforms in the coming age of robotics, and the final piece is a conclusion.

For reference and further exposition, there are four appendices that follow the primary chapters. Appendix A contains the definitive treatment of Hughes' salvo equations, and appendix B provides a procedure for using these equations in fleet planning. Appendix C offers an alternative perspective on the most misused acronym in doctrine, C4ISR.[9] Appendix D shows how the salvo equations can be used to analyze combat power when interchangeable unmanned vehicles are employed. A bibliography and an index complete the text.

This book is also a call to reinvigorate the study of combat theory, with emphasis on the power of operations research to advance new technologies and tactics. Readers should not think themselves poorly educated if this is their first exposure to the term "combat theory." It is little known even within the military academic community, and few are exposed to it at places like the Naval Postgraduate School or the Naval War College. Still fewer researchers would call themselves practitioners in this field. But much of what graced the pages of *Proceedings* during the Golden Age of Tactical Thought could fairly be described as rudimentary combat theory, and a great deal of it eventually found its way into the doctrine and planning of World War II. This book aims to energize a new generation of inquisitive minds to embark on a further development of naval operational art and give rise to a New Golden Age. With new theory, augmented by exercises at sea, mathematical models, simulations, and wargames, the changes imminent in naval warfare from robotics to artificial intelligence to networking might find their proper, practical place in the planning and doctrine of the navies of the future.

1
NAVAL POWER

Power active and power passive; the power to do and the power
to endure; power to exert force and the power to resist it.

—REAR ADM. BRADLEY FISKE
The Navy as a Fighting Machine, 1916

The term "sea power" refers to a nation's maritime prowess. Although
dictionaries define sea power broadly as naval strength, many navalists
prefer to define sea power more finely, as composed of two parts: commercial maritime power and military naval power. Maritime power is straightforward to describe, as shown below. Naval power, by contrast, has always
been somewhat difficult and contentious to characterize.

Many different metrics have been used over the centuries to rate ships.
These include crew size, tonnage, number of guns, throw weight (roughly,
the force per salvo of a gunnery broadside), staying power, and speed or
cruising radius (once engines replaced sails). Each of these is incomplete
and falls short as a measure of a ship's power. Combining measures like
these into a single value for a ship produces inconsistencies and imprecision, and measuring fleets of ships is fraught with misrepresentation, inaccuracy, and subjectivity.

This chapter rectifies this condition. It describes the power of a navy—
specifically, where it comes from and how it is used against other navies.[1]

The chapter starts with a description of a common physical advantage enjoyed by both maritime power and naval power, showing how nations have used this advantage over the history of naval combat. The chapter next explores the different kinds of naval combat power and presents the fundamental model of modern warfare at sea and its implications. After continuing with important questions about current warship construction, the chapter concludes with lessons for planning and admiralship at the fleet level.

MARITIME POWER

Maritime power derives its advantage from buoyancy. Buoyancy is the upward force exerted against an object immersed at the surface of a fluid; in this case the object is a ship's hull, and the fluid is seawater. In our modern age of fast and frequent intercontinental jet flight, the earth can seem quite small to us, and one might overlook the extraordinary benefits of buoyancy. First exploited by oar and sail, next by steam and diesel, and then by nuclear power, buoyancy allows great weights to be borne very long distances with relatively little energy. For even less energy, ships can linger with those weights at their destinations (so long as food or fuel holds out), then with little notice pick up and move great distances again.

But buoyancy has a downside. The same thick fluid that pushes back on a hull to keep a ship afloat also has to be pushed aside as a ship moves forward. Pushing forward creates a wave that pushes back on the ship, and this wave is increasingly difficult to push as the ship moves faster. Because of this effect, fuel-efficient speeds for conventionally designed hulls are quite slow, usually less than twenty knots.[2]

Fuel efficiency doesn't appreciably decrease as hull size increases. In fact, large ships and small ships are fuel efficient at about the same speeds, so for transport purposes, economies of scale drive a preference for large ships over small ships. These economies are so beneficial that, despite its slow speed, hull-borne transport is dramatically superior to air, rail, or truck transport when large cargoes are delivered over great distances.

It is easy to see from the following example how buoyancy allows size to dominate speed. In about 10 hours, the U.S. Air Force's largest airfreight carrier, the C-5, can carry 60 tons of cargo 5,000 nautical miles. To accomplish this impressive feat, however, the C-5 burns about 170 tons of fuel—almost 3 tons of fuel for each ton of cargo. A ship is much slower: the C-5 travels at 500 knots, but a ship typically moves about 15 knots through the water (about 30 times slower than the C-5). It takes the ship some 333 hours (about two weeks) to travel the same 5,000 nautical miles. It would not be unusual, however, for a ship to carry close to 60,000 tons of cargo.[3] At a typical burn rate of 1,000 gals of fuel per hour, a ship would burn nearly 1,200 tons of fuel during the transit—about two hundredths of a ton of fuel for each ton of cargo—a 150-fold improvement in fuel efficiency over airfreight. Notice the trade-off in this example: 30 times slower but 150 times more fuel-efficient. Trade-offs of this order of magnitude between air and sea transport are common, but the payoff is much greater: in this example, 1,000 times more tonnage is moved per trip by sea than by air.

Maritime power is thus mostly about a nation's capability to transport cargo, so metrics that focus on transfer rates of weights or volumes do a fair job of quantifying the maritime part of sea power. Measures of effectiveness like "million ton miles per day" are easy to derive and to employ in the day-to-day management of the sea transport business.

NAVAL POWER

This same logic is the starting point for naval power: buoyancy bestows the same benefits to navies as it does to merchant fleets. A navy can very efficiently carry great loads of military power long distances in large vehicles— this fact separates naval power from other forms of military power. Air power can transport military power much faster but in smaller machines that each carry far less. Armies can constitute much more military power but travel much more slowly and have much smaller units of combat power (the smallest being the soldier itself).[4]

Another unique feature of naval power is that naval vessels not only transport military power but also direct it at enemy targets, right from the ship itself. Fiske saw naval power as first and foremost controllable mechanical power. While this might seem simplistic, his recognition that such tremendous power could be so easily controlled and directed, often by a single actor, still stands as a differentiating feature of a navy. One could infer that this was the genesis of his "admiralship" comment.

Fiske also compared the controllability of naval power to ground power, and his comparison warrants an update. As air power didn't yet exist, he did not make a similar comparison, which ought to be included here. A numbered army has thousands of pieces of heavy equipment, tens of thousands of troops, and a tremendous logistics train. A numbered air force has hundreds of airplanes, prepared airfields, hundreds of pieces of support equipment, thousands of rounds of advanced heavy munitions, and thousands of pilots, aircrew, ground crew, and operations personnel.[5]

Consider the time and effort it would take to project great power from either of these forces, say, six hundred miles. A large army force is lucky to move more than twenty-five miles in an entire day. Army forces also depend on trafficable terrain and a logistics effort that gets increasingly difficult as the army advances.[6] Air forces may get their first increments of combat power on target quickly, but it takes many weeks or months and an extraordinary maintenance and logistics train to complete a major air campaign. Abruptly changing target sets—to one perhaps six hundred miles in a different direction—brings additional challenges. By contrast, a numbered fleet with, say, two aircraft carriers, twenty to thirty combat ships, a dozen or so submarines, about two hundred fixed- and rotary-wing aircraft and its logistics force is self-contained and very mobile, able to bring its entire force six hundred miles in a day, sometimes even fighting its way into position.[7]

NAVAL COMBAT POWER

Navies carry military power for different tasks. Some of it is projected ashore; some of it is applied in offensive and defensive combat against other navies. Early naval combat was as crude as the power carried by the ancients under oar or sail. Ships of opposing navies were defeated by two main techniques: attacking the hulls (by ramming or with fireships) or by attacking the crews. Ships protected against hull attacks by maneuver, by speed, or by increasing the thickness of the hull. The main defense against crew attack was to fight back with the same means.

Gunpowder increased the range at which ships could fight as well as the lethality of their means of destruction. Ships evolved into more complex vehicles, designed mainly for directing and withstanding fires, although crew-on-crew battles were still an important part of naval combat. Ships were not so complex, however, that it was still more profitable to disable a ship and defeat its crew rather than sink its hull. Indeed, capturing and rerigging a ship was, in an old adage, worth "two on the line," since a ship was removed from one combatant's line of battle at the same time it was added to the other's.[8]

The value of muscle, however, decreased with technological innovation. The Machine Age brought steam power, iron hulls, and rifled gunnery to sea. In the eighty or so years before World War II, naval combat was mainly a gunnery duel between machines.[9] This classic form of Machine Age naval warfare was a contest in which combatants applied continuous fire (increments of combat power applied over time) from large-caliber guns against their foes. The total impact, or the throw weight, of all guns against the resistant force of the targeted hull, or staying power, is the primary physical process in a gunnery duel.

The Machine Age also brought a more formalized understanding of naval combat. Just as contemporaries were applying a more scientific approach to management functions in civilian industry, a young naval officer, Lt. J. V. Chase, showed how mathematics could concretely describe these gunnery duels.[10] He recognized that opponents continuously applying combat power to each other over time until one or the other prevailed could be modeled with a series of time-dependent equations. He could then determine the likely winner of a gunnery duel, how many ships of each fleet might be destroyed, and explore such important operational effects as the concentration of fire in line of battle tactics.[11] Chase's work presaged modern operations research techniques, which had to wait until World War II to develop more fully into that discipline.

SALVO WARFARE

From the first days of combat in the Pacific, World War II naval battles featured a new kind of naval combat. Although war at sea was still a clash of competing machines, new vehicles—including submarines and airplanes—applied their combat power differently than ships armed with guns only. With these new types of naval weapons—mines, torpedoes, and bombs—throw weight arrived instantaneously, and the process changed from continuous fire to pulse fire.[12] Even until the beginning of World War II, however, these new weapons were expected to play only a secondary role in warfare at sea, but such battles as Pearl Harbor, Coral Sea, and Midway saw the end of the big guns as a navy's main battery and pulses of power became the focus of fleets.

Just as Chase was able to develop a mathematical model of continuous fire, Hughes was able to apply mathematics to pulse-power interaction. He showed how modern naval combat follows a salvo model: opponents apply a pulse of combat power to each other in an instantaneous salvo exchange. A salvo exchange is an interaction of offensive combat power (e.g., mines, torpedoes, bombs, or missiles) and defensive combat power (e.g., surface-to-air missiles [SAMs], jamming, chaff, decoys). Combat power remaining from these interactions is applied against a target's staying power (the number of hits of a particular weapon that a target can withstand and still be useful for combat purposes).[13]

The salvo attrition equations are the force-on-force equations for pulse combat, which describe the damage (as a fraction of total pre-salvo force) inflicted by one side against another other in a single pulse weapon salvo. The general form for missile combat is

$$\frac{\Delta A}{A} = \frac{\beta B - a_3 A}{a_1 A}, \frac{\Delta B}{B} = \frac{\alpha A - b_3 B}{b_1 B}$$

where

A = number of units in force A.[14]

B = number of units in force B.

α = number of well-aimed missiles fired by each A unit.

β = number of well-aimed missiles fired by each B unit.

a_1 = number of hits by B's missiles needed to put one A out of action.

b_1 = number of hits by A's missiles needed to put one B out of action.

a_3 = number of well-aimed missiles destroyed by each A.

b_3 = number of well-aimed missiles destroyed by each B.

ΔA = number of units in force A out of action from B's salvo.

ΔB = number of units in force B out of action from A's salvo.

What this equation is saying is that the damage to side A is the number of missiles fired by all ships on side B minus the number of those missiles that side A's defense can successfully counter, divided by the total staying power of side A.

Consider two competing three-ship task groups. Assume these ships are identical and have the following characteristics: $\alpha = \beta = 4$, $a_1 = b_1 = 2$, $a_3 = b_3 = 3$. Then after a single salvo,

$$\frac{\Delta B}{B} = \frac{\Delta A}{A} = \frac{4(3) - 3(3)}{2(3)} = \frac{12 - 9}{6} = 0.50, \text{ or } 50\%.$$

Damage of 50 percent means each side will lose half its force, or the equivalent of 1.5 ships. Alternatively, if there is only one ship on side B while side A still has three, then

$$\frac{\Delta B}{B} = \frac{4(3) - 3(1)}{2(1)} = \frac{12 - 3}{2} = 4.50$$

and

$$\frac{\Delta A}{A} = \frac{4(1) - 3(3)}{2(3)} = \frac{4 - 9}{6} = -0.83.$$

This means that B loses its single ship (actually, this 1 ship could be destroyed 4.5 times over) and A loses none (a negative amount of damage means no ships are damaged).

The equations can be iterated to explore sequences of salvos during an ongoing battle. For example, assume the following: $A = B = 3$, $\alpha = 3$, $\beta = 4$, $a_1 = 3$, $b_1 = 2$, $a_3 = 3$ and $b_3 = 2$. Then after a single salvo,

$$\frac{\Delta B}{B} = \frac{3(3) - 2(3)}{2(3)} = \frac{9 - 6}{6} = 0.50$$

and

$$\frac{\Delta A}{A} = \frac{4(3) - 3(3)}{3(3)} = \frac{12 - 9}{9} = 0.33.$$

B loses 1.5 ships and A loses only 1. If the surviving ships attack each other with a second salvo, then

$$\frac{\Delta B}{B} = \frac{3(2) - 2(1.5)}{2(1.5)} = \frac{6 - 3}{3} = 1.00$$

and

$$\frac{\Delta A}{A} = \frac{4(1.5) - 3(2)}{3(2)} = \frac{6 - 6}{6} = 0.$$

B loses its remaining force while A loses none.

What are we to make of results like "destroyed 4.5 times over," "negative damage," or "losing half a ship"? Predicting damage at sea has always been difficult. In the era of big guns, naval officers could estimate how many shells must impact an enemy's ship to exhaust its staying power, but there were frequently unexpected cases of, say, a single lucky round hitting a magazine, inability to control fires or flooding, or disabled interior communications that contributed to a shorter combat life than the equations might prescribe. Given that catastrophic failures occurred with the relatively smaller increments of combat power from guns, it is no surprise that these effects are even more pronounced in salvo warfare. The exact outcomes from salvo exchanges are indeed exceptionally unpredictable.

Salvo equations are best used, then, for comparative analysis rather than predictive analysis. Very useful aspects of war at sea can be explored with this perspective, such as force sufficiency, salvo size selection, the relative strength of offense against a certain defense, fractional exchange ratios, and so on. For example, inflicting 4.5 times more damage than required is one way to overcome the extreme variability in actual results: such a high level of overkill leaves much less to chance than a perfectly sized salvo. For reasons that are discussed later, however, this also suggests that some missiles must be wasted in this effort to reduce uncertainty. Comparative analysis allows this trade-off (overkill versus wasted shots) to be quantitatively addressed.

The usual way that damage is assessed by the salvo equations is pro rata. For example, while in actual combat a three-ship force might incur 50 percent damage a variety of ways (one and a half ships damaged, three ships each with 50 percent damage, two ships with 75 percent damage and one with none, etc.), for comparative analysis the analyst does not make that distinction. The salvo equations are saying that when two forces exchange salvos, then damage per ship ($\Delta B/B$ or $\Delta A/A$) stems from the interaction of three factors: offensive combat power (αA or βB), defensive combat power ($b_3 B$ or $a_3 A$), and staying power ($b_1 B$ or $a_1 A$). We decrement units of offensive combat power by units of defensive combat power and apply the remaining offensive combat power (if there is any) directly to staying power. Since combat power is resident in the hull—perhaps in tubes, launchers, or magazines—any reduction in staying power also incurs a proportional reduction in combat power. So we assume that 50 percent damage means not only that staying power is reduced by half but also that the ability to apply offensive and defensive combat power is reduced by half. The multiple salvo example above shows this approach to proportional damage assessment.

Since analysis with the salvo equations is not meant to be predictive, analysts have to be careful with proportionally attributing damage. In actual combat, a single missile hit on a ship with a staying power of two hits could very likely disable all the ship's combat power, yet the hull could steam on (mission kill); alternatively, the single hit could render the ship dead in the water, but the ship could retain full fighting strength (mobility kill). Exactly where a missile hits a ship's hull or superstructure determines what specific damage is incurred, but since substantial destructive power is delivered with each salvo weapon, a relatively small number of hits can put quite a large ship out of action. After a ship absorbs multiple hits, however, the results of comparative and predictive analysis should converge.

THE SALVO EXCHANGE SET

The comparative-predictive analysis discussion is at the heart of a fundamental condition of salvos: there are very many different outcomes and it is nearly impossible a priori to identify which ones will occur. The salvo exchange set describes all the different outcomes possible in salvo exchanges. The salvo exchange set is defined as

$$S \equiv \{(H \cap D) \cup (H \cap D') \cup (H' \cap D) \cup (H' \cap D')\}$$

where H is the event that offense weapons are properly targeted and will hit their intended targets and D is the event that the defense is successful in destroying inbound weapons.[15]

Until weapons are used, they have combat potential, which in a perfectly efficient system should equal the damage inflicted by their use. If salvo exchanges were perfectly efficient, the only member in the salvo exchange set would be (H $\cap$ D). Since examples of the other three subsets abound, the system is clearly not perfectly efficient. This loss of efficiency is called combat entropy. The four cases resulting from the salvo exchange set are defined below. A brief discussion of each case's contribution to combat entropy is included.

Case 1. *H ∩ D: The defense counters correctly targeted shots.*

This is the most efficient case, although some combat power may be wasted if the defense has an unequal distribution of counterfire and "double-teams" inbound weapons.

Case 2. *H ∩ D': The defense does not counter correctly targeted shots.*

Combat power is wasted by the unsuccessful expense of counterfire. Still worse, unsuccessful "double-teaming" may occur.

Case 3. *H' ∩ D: The defense counters incorrectly targeted shots.*

Combat power is lost by ineffective offensive targeting and by expending of counterfire on a nonthreat. Still worse, unnecessary double-teaming may occur.

Case 4. *H' ∩ D': The defense does not counter incorrectly targeted shots.*

Here combat power is lost by ineffective offensive targeting and ineffective counterfire. Aside from simple misses, two effects—the "weapon-sump effect" (some targets are hit by more than their share of weapons while others do not receive enough hits) and "overkill" (the assignment of more weapons to all targets than are required)—are often operative in this case.

So salvos are obviously complex; what is not generally understood is how complex even "simple" salvo exchanges can be. Consider, for example, three attackers shooting four missiles, each at one defended target. Each missile has the potential to achieve one of the four different outcomes described in the salvo exchange set. This means that for the twelve-missile salvo there are 4^{12} = ~17 million possible outcomes. Not all are equally likely, but it is not possible to determine a priori which will occur, and even a probabilistic prediction can be misleading. One way to manage this fundamental condition of missiles versus missile combat is to look at the distribution of uncertainty in the exchange.

Statistical mechanics already has a measure for the distribution of uncertainty among an ensemble of outcomes in a system, called Gibbs Entropy, S. Since combat entropy is exactly analogous to this entropy concept, we can borrow the standard entropy equation and write our own for combat entropy. The combat entropy, S_C, of a single missile salvo is

$$S_C = -\sum_{i=1}^{N} P_i \times \log P_i$$

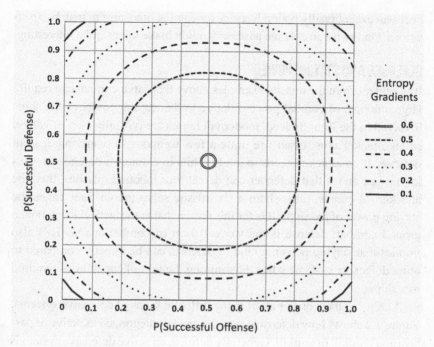

FIGURE1.1 **COMBAT ENTROPY**

where $N = 4$ for all the cases of the salvo exchange set and the P_i values are the probabilities of all H and D combinations (and their complements). Assigning probability values of [0, 1] for both H and D yields the entropy gradients on the topological surface in figure 1.1.[16] Low entropy is found only in the corners (about 5 percent of the surface) because this is where exceptionally good or exceptionally bad performance produces outcomes that comport closely with expectations. The climb from the corner is steep, however, indicating that entropy rises quickly as system performance degrades, even for very good systems. For example, when both H and D are at 0.8, entropy is at about 0.42, more than two-thirds of the maximum of 0.6. A broad, curved dome of high entropy (above 0.4) covers more than half the surface and even includes combinations in which H or D are at very high levels. This shows that sometimes when good performers engage poor performers, outcomes can be very unexpected. This runs counter to intuition and many claims of technical "dominance": an exceptional performer needs an exceptionally poor adversary for combat outcomes to match expectations. Otherwise an average adversary might make things quite interesting.

DEFENSES AND STAYING POWER

It is evident from the missile examples above that salvo combat can require large amounts of combat power relative to the staying power of the ships involved in the fight. Indeed, modern defenses are typically very effective, so an attacker must often fire quite a few weapons to overcome a stout defense. If an attacker needs to get two hits to exhaust a defender's staying power, and if that defender can defeat four inbound missiles, then the attacker, of course, must shoot a six-missile salvo (about three times the staying power of the ship). It is for this reason that at the tactical level, unlike ground combat, defense is the weaker form of combat at sea. This also implies that staying power, a kind of defense, can be directly compared to other defensive systems when determining the mix of capabilities required in a ship.

A ship can have one or all of many different kinds of defensive systems. Figure 1.2 shows how defensive systems can be categorized as active or passive and hardkill or softkill. Generally defined, an active defensive system is one that is directed at a particular threat while a passive defensive system is one that is undirected and employed against a category of threats. Hardkill defenses attempt to destroy a threat while softkill measures seek to confound a threat's attack logic. One interesting feature of the salvo equations is that all modern forms of defense can be included in the calculations, which allow analysts to directly explore trade-offs between them.[17]

	Hardkill	Softkill
Active	antimissile missiles, antimissile guns, etc.	jamming
Passive	armor	stealth, decoys, chaff

FIGURE 1.2 TYPES OF DEFENSE

THE CUBE ROOT RULE

At about the same time that the salvo equations were being formalized at the U.S. Naval Postgraduate School, Lt. Thomas Beall, USN, discovered an ironic aspect of salvo exchanges.[18] His analysis showed that throughout the combat history of steel-hulled ships, the amount of thousand-pound bomb equivalents (TPBEs) of high explosive required to put a ship out of action, on average, was roughly proportional to the cube root of one-thousandth of a ship's tonnage. In other words, about one TPBE can disable or sink a 1,000-ton ship, two TPBEs can take an 8,000-ton ship out of action, three can take out a 27,000-ton ship, and so on. Naval architects have been skeptical about this result because it does not comport with their design analysis. But Beall was observing historical facts. He was not predicting that two TPBEs will put *every* 8,000-ton ship out of action (which is what the design engineer tries to determine). These are two very different approaches. The first asks "what did happen?" and the second asks "what could happen?"

Beall's results are counterintuitive. Navies prefer large ships because they carry more combat power than smaller vessels. Larger ships, therefore, tend to carry more capable defenses. But as tonnage grows, proportionally less combat power is required per ton to put a ship out of action, so defenses must be increasingly capable as tonnage increases. Salvo theory, particularly combat entropy, almost guarantees that even the best defenses will "leak," and as larger salvo sizes are employed to overcome the better defenses of larger ships, more "leakers"—and therefore more damage—will likely result.

But where and how much damage are almost impossible to predict even from nearly identical tactical conditions. There is either great impact, which the combat record tells us follows the cube root rule, or very little impact (those cases where the cube root rule dictates that the ship *should* have been put out of action but was not). The engineer is therefore looking for some average damage value that doesn't exist on a "knife's edge" of combat outcomes. Prudent planners should follow the cube root law when planning salvo engagements.

A BALANCED FLEET?

It is yet another irony that for all the technological effort put into ship design, we have very little direct knowledge of fleet action in the Missile Age. There are some approximate historical examples, such as the naval battle for Okinawa where the kamikaze was used like a cruise missile and 26 ships were sunk, 368 ships were damaged (some beyond repair), and about 9,000 sailors were killed or wounded. Another approximate example is from the Persian Gulf tanker wars from 1981 to 1988, during which Iraq fired about 260 missiles and achieved some 200 hits.[19] These two examples, aside from conveying how devastating missile damage can be, aren't very helpful in gaining a deep understanding of the intricacies of pulse-power combat at sea.

Neither are those cases in which missiles were fired against warships, such as the 1973 Arab-Israeli War, the Royal Navy's experience in the Falklands, or the attack on the USS *Stark*. Although 155 missiles have been fired against warships in the history of war at sea, this sample size is too small, given the high variability of the technical and tactical details between all the cases, such as ship size, crew readiness, defensive capability, missile guidance technology, and so on. Just as in the approximate example, the one consistency was that hits were quite devastating, but otherwise there are not enough apples to compare to apples.

Simulation and wargaming can help us understand modern warfare at sea, but their predictive power is poor. Almost all modern naval simulation and wargaming is stochastic, meaning that their inputs are drawn from averaging probabilistic events. Since historical examples are sparse, the underlying probability distributions are typically based on engineering assessments, test-firings, and professional judgment. In the long years since navies have gone without actual war at sea, it can be fairly argued that these methods have long been captured by corporate bias, headquarters group-think, and budgetary wishful thinking. Indeed, while some decry the salvo equations because they can be used for comparative analysis only, the ability of more mainstream methods to paint a finer picture of naval combat isn't much better.[20]

Comparative analysis, however, still has substantial utility. Consider, for example, the case of a modern guided-missile destroyer, whose main job is to defend itself and other ships with SAMs. These ships have grown increasingly proficient since digital phased-array radars were combined with high-performance SAMs in the 1980s (U.S. Navy ships with the Aegis system are the most advanced example of this combination). Because the radar and missiles are quite difficult to defeat, the worldwide market in antiship cruise missiles (ASCMs) has produced missiles that are faster, smaller (with tinier radar cross-sections), and fly closer to the surface of the sea (confusing some SAM terminal radars and reducing crew reaction time because they fly below the radar horizon). The ASCMs can afford to be smaller since staying power for most combatant ships is much weaker today than in the cases studied by Beall.[21] The result is a kind of equilibrium in missiles, antimissile systems, and hull design that has persisted for many decades.

So we might ask ourselves: If we had another dollar, where should we invest it to improve ship air defense? Is this dollar better spent on improving the phased-array radar? Why not improve the SAMs? Both of these are already exceptional, and further improvements are both very expensive and likely to make ASCMs even smaller and harder to hit. A counterintuitive way to improve the radar and SAMs is to apply the dollar to staying power by armoring the ship. Not only will staying power itself get proportionally more improvement per dollar than can be bought with that same dollar applied to radar and SAMs but, if implemented fleet-wide, this investment will force the worldwide market to build bigger ASCMs. Bigger missiles will be slower and have larger radar cross-sections, which will improve their detection by radar and engagement rate by SAMs. The salvo equations allow one to think through this result directly.

Hughes thought through these and similar questions using the salvo equations and comparative analysis, deriving his concept of tactical stability. Tactical stability is a measure of survivability and combat power, and he maintained that design balance is lost in modern warships with weak staying power. He noted that since staying power is the combat power attribute least affected by particulars of battle, history demonstrates that numerical superiority is the most advantageous force attribute (in other words, numbers count).

ACE (GOAT) FACTOR

The U.S. Air Force has long known about the "Ace Factor": very few fighter pilots score high numbers of kills, and a great many of them never notch a tally. Joseph Bolmarchic put formal rigor to this street wisdom while investigating the distribution of outcomes for a great many varied forms of modern combat.[22] He noted, for example, that the distribution of kills in tank/antitank battles, of tonnage in submarine warfare, and of enemy kills in air-to-air warfare all follow a similar statistical pattern not unlike other types of skewed distributions in human competition (such as power laws, Zipf's law, or other Pareto-like distributions). He noticed a recurring pattern in the distribution of combat outcomes such that a very small number of participants had a very high score, a moderate number had a moderate score, and a very large number had a very small (or even zero) score. He sought not just to describe the shapes of these distributions; he was also looking for distributions that could be described by a single parameter so he could compare the imparity in one set of tactical conditions to the imparity in another, perhaps even from a very different type of combat.

Figure 1.3 shows a typical example, in this case submarine sinkings of Japanese shipping during World War II using postwar Joint Army and Naval Assessment Committee (JANAC) data.[23] The figure shows how just over 60 percent of all submarines accounted for only 20 percent of all

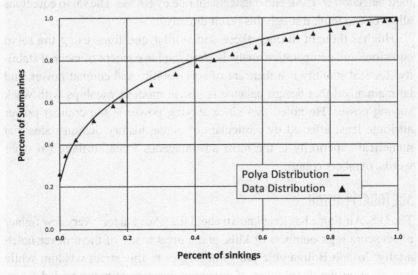

Double Cumulative Distribution
JANAC U.S. Submarine Sinkings of Japanese Ships

FIGURE 1.3 **SKEWED PERFORMANCE IN COMBAT**

sinkings, and 80 percent of submarines accounted for only 40 percent. This meant that the top performing submarines, the top 20 percent, accounted for 60 percent of tonnage sunk. Half of this population (the top 10 percent) accounted for almost 40 percent of all sinkings. Historians will recall that early in the war, many of the best performers were killed in action and the worst performers were relieved of command, so it is interesting to note that, over time, aces and goats both rise and fall from the average population even when individuals in the tails of the distribution are removed from the population.

LESSONS FOR FLEET PLANNERS AND FLAG OFFICERS

In a letter of instruction for Operation Plan No. 29-42 for the defense of Midway, Adm. Chester Nimitz's guidance to his forces stated that "you will be governed by the principle of calculated risk, which you shall interpret to mean the avoidance of exposure of your force to attack by superior enemy forces without good prospect of inflicting, as a result of such exposure, greater damage on the enemy."[24] It is difficult to see how current doctrine and fleet staff training would prepare a modern striking force commander to weigh the risks of today's salvo combat. For example, the guidance of the U.S. Navy's Navy Warfare Publication (NWP) 5-01, *Navy Planning*, is to abandon mathematical calculations and rely on a "rich dialogue" between staff members for a subjective risk assessment.[25]

This chapter addresses the basic physics of how naval power is exchanged between two forces in modern salvo combat, and from this physics comes a perfectly valid mathematical model of the process. Fortunately, the tactical models explained in these pages scale up well to the operational level of war and therefore are valid for the kind of risk-centered decisions that Nimitz expected from his flag officers in wartime. Appendix B provides a general procedure using these equations to concretely assess force-level risk. The numbers, however, only support a decision—they aren't the decision itself, and there are always intangibles that temper what can be made explicit. Nonetheless, in addition to providing an underpinning for the method outlined in appendix B, the concepts and models contained in this chapter substantiate the following lessons for applying naval power for fleet-level decision makers.

1. *Modern Warfare Is Salvo Warfare.* Every staff officer and every decision maker should understand the fundamental physics of how these pulse-power exchanges work. The salvo equations should be employed as part of any calculated risk decisions.

2. *Fire Effectively First (Hughes' maxim).* The salvo equations do not tell the commander and his staff who has a scouting advantage—these quantitative estimates must be made separately. But even without detailed estimates of scouting effectiveness on both sides for different ranges, the equations show quantitatively the reward of getting off the first salvo (or even a partial salvo with longer range missiles) or the severe penalty the force may suffer if the enemy detects and fires first.

3. *Expect Leakers.* Combat entropy is real and will be rampant in salvo exchanges. Even a defense that seems nearly perfect in peacetime testing will be penetrated because of this phenomenon. Combat entropy is not a combat systems failure but the result of the extremely large set of possible events that can occur with even a relatively modest salvo size. Entropy grows larger, and more leakers will occur as salvo sizes get larger. Which ships these leakers hit will also be unpredictable, so consider the impact of hits on various platforms in the force as part of contingency planning.

4. *Shoot Large Salvos.* Outcomes at the fleet level will be very unpredictable (a knife's edge of performance). Advantage in combat with such high levels of uncertainty comes from managing the complexity of the salvo interactions. The surest way to do this is to allocate to your force a pre-ponderance of offensive and defensive combat power, including staying power. Finely tuned salvos between equally matched competitors invite defeat. In *Fleet Tactics*, Hughes exhorts us to "fire effectively first." This is the "effective" part.

5. *Expect to Receive Large Salvos.* Assume that your adversary knows about salvo warfare and will deliver a salvo that they expect will oversaturate your defenses. Given that your adversary knows a substantial amount of combat power will be filtered by your defense, expect that your force will be attacked with much more combat power than you have staying power. You have no inherent advantage in defense over offense like you do in land warfare, but staying power is the combat attribute least affected by technology, the tactical particulars of battle, or states of readiness. Again,

expect leakers. Decoys, softkill, and counter-targeting efforts should be considered in a force-wide plan to decrease the number of missiles assigned to each of your units, but beware: your competitor will size its salvo based on the targets it perceives, not knowing which are valid and which are not, so the use of these techniques will further increase the size of the salvo delivered at your force. This may result in additional leakers.

6. *More Hulls Can Trump More Missiles.* Modern warships are tactically unstable. As ships get larger, they can carry more offensive and defensive combat power, but their staying power does not grow proportionally, so more combat power is put at higher risk. Two four-thousand-ton ships have about the same displacement as one eight-thousand-ton-ship. Suppose the eight-thousand-ton ship can carry twice as much combat power as one of the four-thousand-ton ships; then it carries the same amount as both of them. From the cube root law we know that two hits might put the larger ship out of action, but it would take about 1.6 hits to put each of the two smaller ships out of action. This means that the combat power in the two smaller ships could be 50 percent more survivable. A fleet composed of only larger ships could multiply these decreasing returns throughout the force. Allies may be a ready source of smaller, missile-firing platforms and should be considered in force planning, particularly if your area defense capabilities can protect them.

7. *Human Performance Is Skewed.* After accounting for different technological capabilities between ships and for combat entropy, recognize that human performance adds another source of unpredictability. The historical distribution of human performance in combat indicates that there is no true "average" performance, which you might have observed in peacetime exercises. In fact, there is always a larger population *below* average than above it. For example, if ten ships are assigned to a force, expect that one out of ten will vastly outperform the others, but perhaps six out of ten will be well below par and the other three will be "about average." Peacetime performance is a poor predictor of which specific captains and crews will be in what part of the distribution. If history is any guide, who becomes a hero and who is a goat will likely surprise you. Of course, skew performance distributions are found in fleet staffs, and among flag officer populations as well.

2

SEARCH AND SURVEILLANCE

There is no set of military functions more abused in modern doctrine than those conflated by the acronym C4ISR (command, control, communications, computers, intelligence, surveillance, and reconnaissance). This label is widely used to describe a system in which cutting-edge technologies centralize and automate all the processes for detecting and engaging an enemy. What is frustrating for warfighters is that the terms seem to be redefined almost annually by doctrine writers struggling to keep up with the application of high technology to automated military decision making. In its present state, C4ISR doctrine is a classification science much like early biology, focused more on what things are called rather than on how processes really work. Many writers vie to be the next Carl Linnaeus of command and control, coining new terms and parsing old ones in an increasingly vain attempt to make new jargon stick. But the refreshed doctrine is usually temporary, mainly because the intellectual arguments that support it are about terms of reference, not the inherent nature of military tasks. Those who follow the evolution of the term will recall how the acronym grew from C2, to C3, to C3I, and so on. Within the last few years, doctrine has had to suffix a new acronym, PED (processing, exploitation, and dissemination), because so much of the basic work of finding and attacking an enemy had leaked out of the original parade of incomplete categorizations.

This chapter reduces C4ISR doctrine for operational naval warfare to the two primary detection functions, search and surveillance. It explains how each is a distinct process that must be planned and managed at the fleet level quite differently from the other. The chapter also describes common misconceptions about how search and surveillance information is presented to fleet staff and flag officers. Search theory is discussed, as well as operational-level guidance for how to treat lost or evasive targets. The chapter also specifies how fleet planners can use nontechnical methods to improve search and surveillance, and then concludes with lessons for fleet planners and flag officers.

Appendix C provides important technical context and should be read before reading further in this chapter. It shows how fleet decision making is poorly served by C4ISR terms so long as they are consigned to an automated, centralized command-and-control system of systems. The goal of this chapter and its associated appendix is not to redefine C4ISR but—through systematic examination—to greatly clarify the topic for fleet-level decision makers. It is hoped that this formal approach will have the same simplifying effect on C4ISR doctrine that scientific discoveries like genetics, photosynthesis, and molecular chemistry had on modern biology.

THE FLEET TARGET SET

Just as naval power is different from that of the other armed services, the detection environment and the nature of the targets within it are substantially different from those encountered by the other military branches. For example, while air and ground forces might argue that they are "all-weather" forces, what they actually mean is that they can perform in an "instrument-only" environment of poor visibility, cloud cover, or heavy precipitation. Naval forces, by contrast, can still perform most missions (except those that are aviation-centric) in up to Tropical Cyclone Category 1 conditions, so they must succeed at their detection tasks in some of the most extreme atmospheric circumstances imaginable.

Even without such severe weather challenges, the maritime environment can still significantly reduce the performance of detection systems: targets can be intermittently obscured by high waves, radar can be attenuated by heavy sea spray, and water temperature differences can make even a nearby submarine invisible to sonar. Thankfully, the naval environment can increase detection performance as well. For example, a ship at sea far from prominent land features will enjoy very long-range detection of aircraft at appropriate altitudes, atmospheric ducting at sea can provide over-the-horizon radar detections, and certain other water temperature conditions can provide extremely long-range sonar detection.

Table 2.1 shows how the targets and the means of detection within these conditions create a very high-dimensional set of detection challenges and opportunities.[1] The columns represent the types of targets that go to sea (or, in the case of information and space, support a navy's fight). The rows portray the numbers of each kind of target one should expect, the speed at which these targets travel, their primary means of detection, and the decision time it takes to prosecute a target once it is initially detected. Because, for example, there is a big difference between the speed of sound in water and the speed of radio frequency waves in air, there are great variations between the detection methods used against submarines and those used against aircraft, requiring naval commanders to have both high- and slow-speed decision processes. Similarly, a battle staff at sea needs the capability to manage a high number of friendly, enemy, and neutral air targets at the same time that they need to manage high detail on a small number of sub-surface contacts. Often the detecting platform is in neither the air medium nor the subsurface medium but in a surface ship operating across three media. These challenges and opportunities are more profound at media boundaries, and navies must, of course, operate across all media.

TABLE 2.1 **DIMENSIONS OF NAVAL SURVEILLANCE AND SEARCH**

	Air	Surface	Submarine	Information	Space
Numbers	10s-100s	1s-10s	1s	1,000s	1s
Speed	100 kts	10 kts	10 kts	100,000 kts	1,000 kts
Detection mode	EM/RF/EO	EM/RF/EO	Acoustic	electronic	EM/RF/EO
Decision time	seconds	minutes	minutes to hours	seconds to days	hours to days

SEARCH

Search is a detection process in which a detector purposefully moves a field of view to initiate detection. Search is a proactive process, much like police detective work. Examples of search include an escort detached from a convoy to find a nearby submarine, a surface group combing an area for enemy surface craft, or a submarine cued from a surveillance system looking for a target within an area of uncertainty (AOU). Sensors can be active or passive, such as an airborne search radar or a shipboard radio-frequency detector. What sets searching apart from surveillance is the purposefulness of the detection effort. While a surveillance system maintains a fixed field of view and approaches every target equally, search involves a moving field of view in which the searcher's movement and the sensor are tuned to target characteristics. Often time is a driving factor.

Importantly, search efforts treat negative information as information about a target.[2] In fact, one of the techniques for a successful coordinated search is to build a probability map that shows which regions of a search area are likely to contain the target and which are not. At the start of the search, every region is considered just as likely to contain the target as any other. Continued search without detection suggests that regions already searched are now less likely to contain the target, while those yet to be searched are more likely. In this way, negative information allows commanders to manage their search, directing assets away from lower probability regions to those with higher probability.

SURVEILLANCE

Surveillance is a detection process in which a detector stares at a prescribed field of view, relying primarily on the purposeful movement of a target to initiate detection. Surveillance is a reactive process, much like a police officer on a stakeout. Examples of surveillance include an air defense ship on station, a maritime patrol aircraft in a fixed orbit, or a satellite focusing on a swath of earth's surface. The sensor can be active, like an air search radar, or passive, like a listening array of sonar hydrophones. Surveillance is often performed as a coarse-scale, continuous inspection of a wide region, which is then followed by a fine-scale, cued prosecution. An important feature of coarse-scaling in surveillance is that there is a kind of "equality" of targets since detectors (human or electronic sensors) process all potential targets in the field of view through the same apertures. This can lead to false or failed detections.[3]

More importantly, surveillance systems provide very limited negative information about targets. Since surveillance systems can merely point out the apparent absence of a target in a fixed field of view, not much more than that fact informs the detector.

SEARCH THEORY

There is a well-defined theory of search, but before embarking on the mathematics of search theory, it is helpful to examine a more concrete model perfectly analogous to search activities—mowing a lawn. Most people mow their lawn with some kind of pattern, perhaps a collapsing square or back and forth with overlapping swaths. These perfect patterns are the most efficient way of mowing. Will all the grass get cut? It depends on how sharp the mower's blades are and if there are no gaps in the pattern. What if, however, the person mowing the lawn has no perfect pattern? What if they mow, say, in a random direction for some amount of time, turn to another random direction and mow for the same amount of time, and so on. The amount of grass cut by both methods (given that both blades are equally sharp) is exactly the same. The difference is that the perfect pattern cuts the grass in the shortest time, while it can take an infinite amount of time to randomly cut the grass. Counterintuitively, early in the grass-cutting process both methods perform about the same (in amount of grass cut and grass cut per unit time). The methods soon diverge, however, as the random grass-cutter starts to re-mow previously cut patches. Not too long after the perfect mower finishes, the random mower will be mostly done with the lawn but is destined to re-mow toward infinity, waiting to randomly return to the last isolated blades skipped in the process.

The mathematics of search theory formalizes a similar process in the classic random search model. Assume a target is present and its position is uniformly distributed in area A. Assume the searcher detects the target with certainty when it is within range r and never beyond. The sweep width, W, equals $2r$. Assume the searcher's path is random in A. Divide the searcher's total path length, L, into n segments of equal length, L/n, as in figure 2.1.

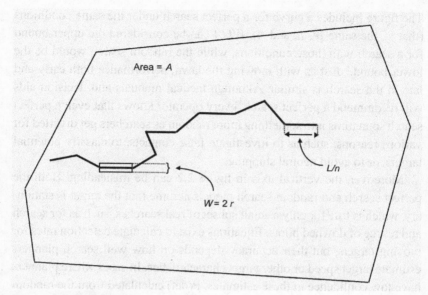

Area = A

L/n

W = 2 r

FIGURE 2.1 RANDOM SEARCH

Let B be the event that the target is within detection range in the first segment—that is, the target is within the area WL/n centered on the first segment. The probability that event B occurs is

$$P(B) = WL/An.$$

By similar arguments, we can calculate the probability of detection over the entire segment L as

$$P(det_{total}) = 1 - e^{-WL/A},$$

which can be easily determined from operational values for r, L, and A.[4] Since L is related to time, we can plot P(det) against time, allowing us to address operational considerations such as how much time it might take to search to a given level, what percent of the search is completed by a specific time, or how much sooner other assets (such as a faster searcher or one with a wider search width) would find the target, and so on. Figure 2.2 shows both a perfect search and a random search plotted as P(det) versus time.

The figure includes a curve for a perfect search under the same conditions (that is, the same W, L, and A). WL/A can be considered the upper bound for a search with those conditions, while the random search would be the lower bound.[5] Just as with mowing the lawn, performance both early and late in the search is similar. Although tactical manuals and decision aids will recommend a perfect search, every operator knows that even a perfect search soon turns into something more random as searchers get diverted for various reasons, such as to investigate false contacts, to classify potential targets, or to avoid neutral shipping.

Moreover, the vertical axis in figure 2.2 can be misleading. Both the perfect search and random search models assume that the target is stationary, which is true for only a small subset of real searches, such as for search and rescue of downed pilots. Equations exist to calculate detection rates for moving targets, but their accuracy depends on how well search planners estimate target speed or other target characteristics. In cases where planners have low confidence in these estimates, P(det) calculated from the random search algorithm is used as a proxy for percent of area coverage and uses the upper and lower bounds to determine which assets to employ. Since L is also related to speed, sweep rate (area swept per unit time) can help identify the searcher that provides the best coverage. For a surface search, for example, sweep rate favors aviation assets since their detection ranges are comparable to surface forces, yet they search at speeds up to ten times faster. An interesting feature of searches involving moving targets is that targets themselves have a kind of sweep rate (an interaction rate with the searcher based on range and speed), so if all other considerations are equal, a higher speed target might be more quickly detected than one at slower speed (or stationary).

Figure 2.3 shows the calculations for a notional search problem. A typical operating area for naval operations would be perhaps 400 nm by 400 nm (160,000 nm^2). Consider three destroyers deployed together in this area conducting a visual search with their helicopters at an operational speed of 15 knots (the helicopters can, of course, fly faster, but they must stay within line-of-sight communications range of the destroyers, so the group speed is 15 knots). Assume the search range for the helicopters is out to 60 nm (making their sweep width 120 nm). With these inputs, the perfect search

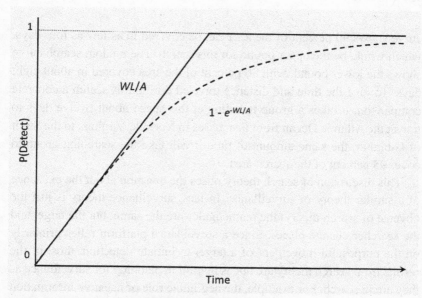

FIGURE 2.2 PERFECT SEARCH VERSUS RANDOM SEARCH

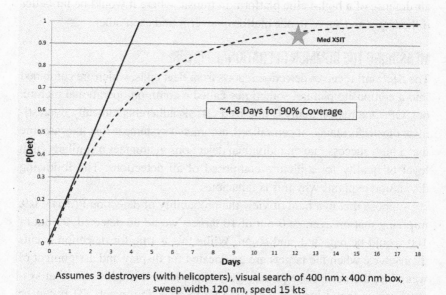

Assumes 3 destroyers (with helicopters), visual search of 400 nm x 400 nm box,
sweep width 120 nm, speed 15 kts

FIGURE 2.3 A NOTIONAL SEARCH PROBLEM

curve shows 90 percent of the area can be covered in as few as four days, which would be the upper bound for this search. The random search curve shows the lower bound, with 90 percent of the area covered in about eight days. To give the time and distance traveled during this search a concrete comparison, it takes a group traveling at this speed about twelve days to transit the Atlantic Ocean from fleet bases in Norfolk, Virginia, to the Strait of Gibraltar, the same amount of time it will take the searching group to cover 95 percent of the search area.

This discussion of search theory raises the question about the existence of a similar theory of surveillance. In fact, surveillance theory is just the obverse of search theory: the mathematics are the same, but the target and the searcher change places. Since a surveillance platform relies primarily on the purposeful movement of a target to initiate detection, most of the results from search theory are not as helpful in planning for surveillance as they are in search. For example, the negligible role of negative information in surveillance has already been discussed, and one can only infer what an enemy's search rate might be. Moreover, there are many scenarios, such as air defense of a high-value platform in transit, where it would be far better if the target and surveillance platform never found each other.

MEASURING THE COMMON OPERATIONAL PICTURE

The fleet staff receives detection reports from fleet units, which are combined into a composite picture, sometimes called a common operational picture, or COP. One reason many centralized C4ISR adherents radically overestimate the performance of centralized, automated systems is that they assume that a high success rate on individual detections guarantees a similarly high level of quality for a picture composed of all detections. The following discussion explains why this is fallacious.

Suppose that in a field of view the probability of detection P(det) = 0.9, implying that on average 9 out of 10 targets would be detected, 90 out of 100 would be detected, and so on. While this is true for detection events themselves, when the targets are geolocated for display and assignment of weapons, the composite picture gets much more complex. Combat systems assign target location error (TLE) to detection events. TLE can be calculated from many factors, including sensor acuity, detection platform navigation error, time since last detection, target speed, and so on. TLE is typically represented as an area of uncertainty, AOU (or, sometimes, a containment ellipse), which bounds the region in which a target is assumed to lie with a given probability.

Most people unfamiliar with probability theory assume that a COP with 10 targets (each of which is within an AOU of 0.9) has itself a 0.9 level of accuracy (in other words, *all* the targets are within their 0.9 AOUs). This assumption can be tested with the binomial probability law, which defines the probability of k successes in n attempts at success when the probability of success for each event is p.[6] From the binomial probability law, we can calculate that the probability that *all* targets are within their 0.9 AOUs is actually 0.9^{10}, or 0.349. So while many operators might assume this calculation should be somewhere near point A in figure 2.4, in reality the composite accuracy of the COP is near point B.

How can the composite accuracy of the COP get closer to 0.9? The AOUs must each increase in accuracy by an order of magnitude, to 0.99.

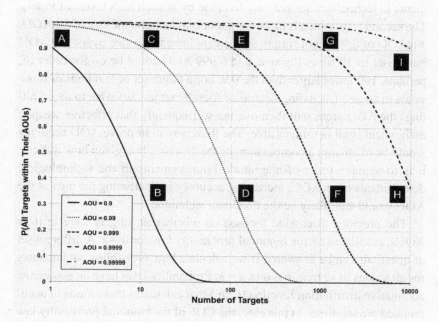

FIGURE 2.4 **BINOMIAL PROBABILITY CURVES FOR** $n = k$

Again, from the binomial probability law, the probability that all 10 targets are within 0.99 AOUs is $0.99^{10} = 0.904$, or near point C in figure 2.4. But what if the number of targets is increased by an order of magnitude, to 100? The probability that all 100 targets are within their AOUs is $0.99^{100} = 0.367$ (point D). To get a 100-target COP back to a composite accuracy of 0.9, one must increase the accuracy of each AOU yet another order of magnitude, to 0.999 (point E). The probability that all events occur is $0.999^{100} = 0.905$. And so on, to points F, G, H, and I.

The main difficulty with chasing COP accuracy in this manner lies in the fact that, as a practical matter, increasing the accuracy of an AOU is exceptionally nontrivial, with technological challenges and negative operational implications. Increasing the accuracy of an AOU from 0.9 to 0.99, for example, can be accomplished only three ways. The first would be by manipulating one or all of the detection-related factors that determine the size of the AOU (such as increasing sensor acuity or decreasing navigation error). While this is indeed possible, such order-of-magnitude improvements in technology are not easy to come by at such high levels of P(det). The second way, which is more common, is to increase the size of the AOU. An AOU of 0.99 is not simply a 9 percent increase in size over a 0.9 AOU but closer to 10 times the size, and 0.999 AOU could be on the order of, perhaps, 100 times larger than the 0.9. For a target set of hundreds or thousands of targets (including neutral or friendly targets we wish to avoid hitting) the AOU areas will then overlap so frequently that effective weapon assignment is all but impossible. The third way to improve AOU accuracy would be to attempt a combination of the first two, but, given how difficult it is to achieve order-of-magnitude improvements in the technological determinants of an AOU, increasing accuracy by increasing the area of the AOU would still likely be the dominant technique.

The previous discussion focused on whether *all* targets were in their AOUs, calculated by the binomial probability law for $n = k$. A different set of questions can be answered if we calculate how probability accumulates for all values of n, from $n = 0$ to $n = k$. Probability laws have an associated cumulative distribution function (CDF) that calculates these kinds of accumulated probabilities. In this case, the CDF of the binomial probability law calculates the probability that there are n or more of k targets in their AOUs.

Subtracting the value of the CDF from 1.0 will show the probability that *at least* a certain number *n* of targets are in their AOUs.

Using this perspective, as target sets get larger, what kind of COP should we expect with 0.9 AOUs? Examine figure 2.5, which shows the upper end (greater than 50) of the CDF values for 100 targets and 0.9 AOUs. This chart tells a different and more operationally relevant story than the previous discussion. Following the curve from left to right, note that we can be almost certain that at least 80 of the targets are in their AOUs (which means, though, there is at least *some* uncertainty about 20 targets). At the 0.9 level (the original expectation for the COP), about 85 of the targets are likely in their AOUs, although we are somewhat less certain about that fact, plus we are now 90 percent sure that at most 15 targets are out of their AOUs. Following the curve to the right, we see that we are 50 percent sure that 90 targets are in their AOUs and 50 percent sure that 10 targets are not in their AOUs. So our original "9 out of 10 in their AOUs" expectation is at best a 0.50 probability.

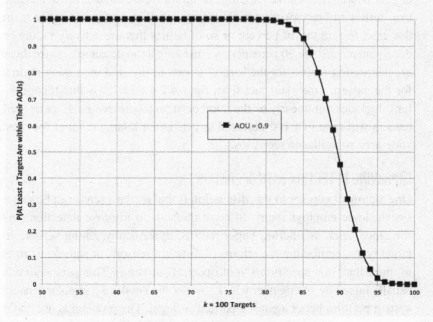

FIGURE 2.5 **PROBABILITY THAT AT LEAST *n* TARGETS ARE WITHIN THEIR AOUs**

One can derive some conclusions from the CDF representation. The first is that at the upper end of expectations of COP accuracy, the certainty of those expectations drops off precipitously. Second, as this happens, the operational implication is not that "COP accuracy"—some abstract measure of information quality—has decreased, but that something decidedly physical has happened: a real number of targets are not where they are expected to be and therefore cannot be engaged effectively. More troubling is the fact that the COP cannot tell us exactly which ones are not where they should be, so confidence in the COP should be much lower than a "COP accuracy" measure would suggest. This shows the weakness of such abstract information-theoretic measurements. Finally, the CDF for 0.9 AOUs tells us that while some small percent of target representations will not likely be accurate, a very large percentage will. While this might seem like a very good outcome, it can be exploited by a clever adversary against a surveillance system. Cover, concealment, deception, and decoy operations are designed to produce exactly this result: to clutter a picture with false or invaluable targets while preventing location of the real, most valuable targets. Moreover, neutral shipping and air traffic are much more detectable than furtive military platforms. So the real challenge of surveillance is, in this case, to find the 10 percent or so of targets that are actively hiding or deceiving among the 90 percent or so that are all too detectable, since there are decreasing returns for the hardest targets to find and increasing returns for the easiest. One clear fact from figures 2.4 and 2.5 is that this problem degrades nonlinearly as the number of targets increases. Experienced readers will note that 100 potential targets is not a large number for most wide-area surveillance scenarios.

IMPROVING DETECTION WITH OPERATIONS

One argument counter to this discussion is that modern sensor and combat system logic employs many different methods to improve detection performance, such as filtering target returns, dynamically tuning sensors to target types, combining the returns of different sensors, or sensing a target in more than one spectrum ("multispectral" sensing). This perspective is usually raised by an engineer who knows how to make a particular sensing system perform better against a particular target. The problem is not that it is hard to make *each* detection better but to make *all* detections better. The discussion above shows that this is very difficult for even very high levels of performance (AOUs of 0.9 and higher), which are already near the best that all these techniques can provide. Even if engineers can achieve better results at these performance extremes, the cost and effort will likely be prohibitive for the return on each new target more accurately located.

How else might systems or operators improve the performance of a detection system, particularly one that is already technologically advanced? One technique, used predominantly in air surveillance, is to map out the regularities in the field of view so that operators can focus on irregular behavior. For example, modern air defense combat systems allow operators to enter published airline traffic route data into target identification logic routines and display systems. Alerts are provided when targets deviate from these routes so that operators can provide more discernment to the deviant contacts. Such measurement of ambient signals allows for detection of anomalies—if not already included in surveillance system logic—to be accomplished subconsciously by operators: they filter out the ambient signal and key on anomalies.

Inducing or leveraging an operational pattern can improve the performance of a detection system. Placing a field of view across a strait or positioning it at the entrance to a cul de sac (like a narrow gulf or basin) are obvious techniques, which can be further leveraged if other fleet activities (such as active search) drive potential targets toward the field of view. More advanced maneuvers would cause potential targets to cycle multiple times through a field of view. For example, sending a high-value unit (HVU) through, say, the Celebes Sea and Makassar Strait toward the Strait of Malacca can cause an enemy to cross a field of view placed at the Luzon Strait. Reversing the movements of the HVU at the appropriate time can drive enemy targets back through this field of view. While a thinking enemy might eventually divine the purpose of the HVU's apparent navigational irregularities, this effect might still be achieved enough times to accomplish the goal of the detection effort.

One of the most important decisions in a detection effort is to decide what to do when detection becomes ineffective. There are three cases to consider. The first case involves targets that appear only briefly. This could be the result of surveillance in a medium through which each detection is quite difficult (like the undersea medium), or in which a target signal intermittently rises above the ambient signal (such as a high-speed surface target). This latter example is analogous to how quick and nimble prey (like rabbits or deer) avoid their predators: they briefly reposition with speed and then blend back into the environment with their camouflaging coats. The second case is when the AOU is insufficient for engagement, but no further detection efforts can improve it. The third case is when surveillance needs to produce a target for the current mission but has failed to do so; that is, minimizing the time-to-detect becomes an important driver.

EVASION

The notional search problem in figure 2.3 shows how long it can take to find a target in a large area. Targets, of course, prefer not to be found and, if found, want to get lost and stay lost as quickly as possible. How quickly might that target get lost once it is found? One result from an underdeveloped branch of search theory, called "hider theory," can be employed to address this question. Consider the same 400 nm × 400 nm search area.[7] Naval history is replete with examples of searchers completely losing contact within just a few moments, perhaps even after tracking the target for days or weeks. These lost detections might be caused by inattention, intermittently poor atmospherics, sensor casualties, evasive target motion, decoys, or any combination of these and other operational realities.

The insert chart in figure 2.6 shows how quickly a circle containing a lost target can grow each hour the target remains lost. Recognizing that the target can evade in any direction and assuming an evasion speed of r, we can use the well-known formula for the area of a circle, $A = \pi r^2$, to calculate the size of the area that feasibly contains the target. As shown in the inset, in one hour, this area grows by 100 percent. In the second hour, this area grows *another* 300 percent, while in the third hour, the area grows another 125 percent. By the fourth hour, the rate of growth starts to slow, but only because the size of the total area that might contain the target has already become quite large. The main chart in figure 2.6 shows that for evasion speeds of 15, 30, and 45 knots it takes between five and eight hours for this

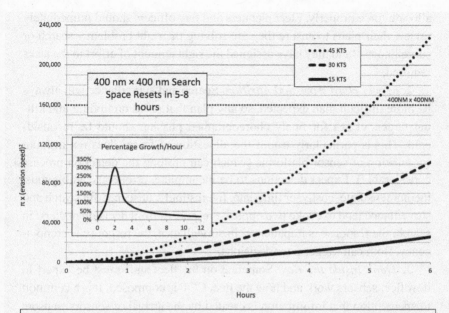

Targets are found in days, lost in minutes, and either regained in hours...
...or they are not found again for days

FIGURE 2.6 **A NOTIONAL EVASION PROBLEM**

area to grow to the size of the original 400 nm × 400 nm search area, resetting the search problem completely. In other words, it can take days to find a target, and that target can be lost in minutes. If the target is not regained in hours, it can once again take days to find the target.

LESSONS FOR FLEET PLANNERS AND FLAG OFFICERS

It would be nice if all the promises of network-centric warfare would come true, but at least for now, fleets should be resigned to the fact that there is no crystal ball for search and surveillance, particularly against a clever enemy. The following points should guide senior staff decision making until such time, if ever, that advanced C4ISR systems provide all the capabilities they have advertised.

1. *Solve the Right Problem.* Most operational plans do not distinguish between search and surveillance. It follows, then, that these plans do not

allocate force properly. Fleet planners and flag officers should immediately review their plans to ensure they are solving the right problem—search or surveillance—and they have assigned the right amount of effort to the tasks required.

2. *Expect Hard Work and Attrition.* Search and surveillance will always be more difficult than expected, so any plan that relies on finding and killing targets at sea for finely choreographed phasing should be reconsidered. This is particularly true if the allocation of forces does not account for attrition of sensor platforms (which can prolong the detection process considerably). Expect detections to be incomplete, erroneous, ambiguous, incommensurate, costly, or time-late. Interestingly, unsuccessful search and surveillance tend to evoke two opposite responses from decision makers: in search, the response is impatience; in surveillance, the response is complacency. Both can trigger poor decisions.

3. *Think Inside the Box.* Someone on the fleet staff must be expert in how fleet sensors work and how the fleet COP is composed. It is a common misperception that information is created by the arrival of sensors: sensors simply sample the environment for phenomena and report what they see based on logic not readily apparent to operators. Those charged with looking inside the fleet's black boxes should educate the force on how sensors and fusion processes treat the most likely threat platforms and, just as important, how they might fail.

4. *Detection Is a Competition, Not a Process.* In combat, there is a "ground truth" that neither competitor truly sees and of which each has only their own perception. There is a fight for these perceptions, and competitors will make it hardest to find those assets they wish to keep hidden while doing their best to clutter the environment with low-value targets, decoys, jamming, or neutral platforms. In war at sea, search and surveillance platforms are also their adversary's targets, and both sides are attempting to fix the position of the other, yet remain unlocated by their enemy. Fleet staffs and flag officers should put the same level of competitive thought and two-sided planning into the sensor fight as they put into planning their salvos. For the most valuable enemy platforms, planners should develop procedures for prosecuting lost contact and consider keeping a ready reacquisition force in reserve.

5. *Human Performance Is Skewed.* Just as in the salvo fight, fleet planners and flag officers should expect that a small number of platforms and decision makers will perform superbly in search and surveillance and a moderate number will perform "about average," but most will perform below peacetime expectations. Identification mistakes can be prevalent early in a campaign (visual identification is particularly error-prone), but inaccuracies of all types could make the COP very suspect. Over time, a staff's natural inclination is to learn whose reports to trust, but this can create biases that give some reports more—and some reports less—credence than they deserve.

3
LOGISTICS AND MANEUVER

The oceans are vast, as anyone can see if they flip over a globe to the South Pacific or peer out the window from 35,000 feet on a transatlantic flight. The sailor, however, has a different perspective on this vastness. Hundreds of miles from the nearest landfall on the fantail of a destroyer lolling between swells, standing just feet from the ocean itself, every sailor feels a special isolation: that a fire, mechanical failure, or contamination of fuel tanks can leave sailor and crew at the mercy of the elements for days until help can arrive. The ocean can surely batter a wounded or thirsty ship during peacetime, but a damaged ship at war without food, fuel, and bullets is in a uniquely grim condition. The crew cannot by itself awaken the great power that lies within, and even a much smaller enemy could appear at any moment and easily slay a vulnerable giant.

The oceans are also small. There are many examples of a naval force that—after weeks of tedious transit over a very wide expanse—unwittingly stumble on an enemy force and find themselves thrust headlong into brief, furious, and brutal combat. Of course, well-directed fleets ought to avoid the need for short-notice heroics, but naval history has too many such battles that arose out of seemingly spacious sea room.

This chapter is about logistics and maneuver in oceans that are both vast and cluttered. Logistics protects a fleet against the isolation of great distances, and maneuver positions a fleet for success against an enemy in a crowded sea. Maneuver then allows a force—either in lieu of or after battle—to withdraw to the safety of a lonely sea. Logistics, in turn, slakes an expended fleet's thirst for fuel and hunger for ordnance so that maneuver can redirect the force to fight again. Logistics and maneuver are in this way inextricably united, interdependent, and complementary in well-planned and executed naval warfare.

LOGISTICS

A Napoleonic maxim of ground combat is that an army marches on its stomach. More than anything else, troops need to stop and eat to continue to move and fight. Although modern troops usually ride in vehicles, an army must now feed its machines as well; tanks, armored personnel carriers, and trucks can't get too far ahead of their supply train without pausing for fuel tank refills to catch up. And troops still need to eat. Ground logistics is a challenging process by which large stockpiles of supplies are distributed in small units of issue to large numbers of small combat entities, perhaps every two to three days. A ground force that outruns its supplies is in quite a precarious state—which is why a field army moves only about twenty-five miles each day it is on the move.[1]

Naval forces are much less tied to a logistics train. Even in Napoleon's time, the biggest limitation to a ship's cruising range was fresh food and water for the crew.[2] Shot and powder were supplied only when depleted (and these could be purchased overseas or captured from a prize), and repairs from heavy weather or enemy action (that could not be fixed at sea) could be completed at any friendly port. After many months, particularly in the tropics, a ship had to be careened for hull-cleaning, but otherwise the force could sail far and wide with little dependence on a dedicated logistics scheme. Note that there were really only three kinds of support that ships required: regularly consumed supplies such as the crew's daily ration, episodic support such as refilling magazines or repairing minor damage, and major, long-term maintenance. While modern joint forces use a highly specialized categorization and distribution system for ten classes of supply (with numerous subclasses), modern naval forces still require these three kinds of support.

The shift from sail to steam brought extraordinary changes to navies worldwide. In addition to sweeping changes in weapons, control technology, tactics, and naval architecture, new navy machines brought daily fuel requirements, which in turn have important strategic implications. A modern destroyer has perhaps a quarter-million gallons of fuel on board, which can power its engines for about five thousand miles. This ship can cover much of the earth's surface, so long as it has a place to refuel every week or so. Fueling stations thus became a primary strategic consideration for navies of the late nineteenth century. In peacetime, the same coal sold to merchant ships could be bought from contractors, but as naval competition between the industrialized nations became more intense, obtaining and securing exclusive coaling stations were critical strategic problems as well. As navies secured fueling stations, it was natural for those stations to also serve the other needs of a fleet: regular consumables (like food for the crew), episodic consumables (like ammunition), intermittent repair services, and major maintenance. Over time some of these stations became permanent operating bases, with fixed infrastructure of warehousing, modern piers, fuel farms, drydocks, foundries, cranes, and machine shops.

The U.S. Navy first conducted wartime refueling at sea in 1917, which obviated the need to return to a station or collier for routine coaling. Refueling at sea was made much easier by the conversion from coal to oil that had begun at the turn of the century, and the requirement to replenish fuel oil on the order of about once a week remains to this day. Table 3.1 shows approximate distances from fleet concentration areas to various theaters in which the U.S. Navy routinely operates. Roughly speaking, a destroyer traveling at twenty knots will burn about 10 percent of its fuel capacity and travel about five hundred miles a day. So a ship transiting from Hawaii to Korea will therefore take about six days, arriving with about 40 percent fuel on board. Similarly, a ship traveling from the U.S. West Coast to the same destination will need to refuel during the transit.

By the end of World War II, it was common for food and ammunition as well as fuel to be delivered directly at sea, so although the fleet no longer needed to return to bases for these necessities, bases were still needed to stockpile them for a fleet of special-purpose service craft to deliver at sea. Naval logistics, then, can be ashore at traditional naval bases, at sea with replenishment at sea techniques, or even in shelter, like at the mammoth logistics base at Ulithi atoll in World War II, which offered a combination of both.

THE POWER OF BASES

Chapter 1 discusses different kinds of naval power: machine power, offensive combat power, defensive combat power, and staying power. Since they provide for all these kinds of naval power, naval bases are sources of naval power. They provide the fuel, feed the crew, and repair the equipment of the machines that transport and direct naval power; they also deliver the ammunition that constitutes offensive and defensive combat power, and they maintain or repair damage to hulls, restoring staying power.

Naval bases are not simply sources of naval power to prepare for a fight; they regenerate naval power after a fight. Naval bases restore combat power for ships that can immediately return to combat. For those ships that are too damaged to fight on, naval bases perform an important triage role. While operational timelines usually rule out regeneration of staying power for the most badly damaged ships, skilled engineers with the appropriate infrastructure can diagnose which mission kills or near-misses can be repaired quickly enough to return to the fight from those who have become operational kills (that is, unavailable for the current campaign).[3] Salvage and towing assets sufficient to recover major units after combat operations must be included in the fleet inventory, and recovery operations need to be built into operational logistics plans.[4] It has been a very long time since the world's navies have had to seriously consider what to do about platforms

TABLE 3.1 **NOTIONAL DISTANCES TO THEATERS OF INTEREST**

Theaters of Interest	Distances (nm)*
U.S. East Coast to Mediterranean Sea	4,300
U.S. East Coast to Persian Gulf	8,400
U.S. West Coast to Korea	5,300
U.S. West Coast to Persian Gulf	11,000
Hawaii to Korea	3,200
Hawaii to Persian Gulf	8,900
Intratheater 1	1,000
Intratheater 2	2,000

* Distances are representative, not policy-approved distances used for
  force structure/deployment policy calculations.

crippled and adrift due to combat damage. When should a severely damaged ship be recovered, and when should it simply be scuttled or sunk? In a peacetime navy, the latter may seem like unthinkable acts, but more than once in World War II they were the only bitter choices of leaders at sea.

MANEUVER

For ground and joint combat, maneuver seems to hold an almost mystical place in history and in doctrine. A surprise outflanking by a stolen march, clever feints followed by sharp attacks elsewhere, and timely and swift commitment of a force held in reserve are classic examples of the great advantages that properly choreographed maneuver can provide. Ground forces accrue great power through a stout defense in a terrain-limited fight for an important piece of land. Masterful maneuver is often the only way that a ground force commander might overcome the power inherent in defense ashore.

Naval forces, by contrast, have no such power in the defense and are not so fettered by land and location, and current doctrine currently relegates maneuver to a lesser role in combat at sea. This has not always been true. For centuries, tactical maneuver at sea—such as seizing favorable winds for a fight, "Crossing the T," or cutting the line of battle—was the very essence of tactics. But modern missile combat with long-range search and surveillance has dramatically increased the range at which fleets interact, and tactical maneuver is now a lost art that navies will need when oceans grow small.

Perhaps the most direct way to reestablish skill in naval maneuver at all levels of war is to reexamine the terms for maneuver from Fiske's day: cruising, approach, and attack. These correspond very well to strategic, operational, and tactical maneuver, yet their names, for sailors, are much more descriptive. Consider the force deploying from point A in figure 3.1. This force likely starts in a low-threat environment, just beginning a long-range transit to a theater of operations. The force is most concerned with ferrying combat power to theater, so it is performing "strategic lift," leveraging buoyancy to efficiently carry as much as possible as far as possible. Operational security (OPSEC, denying information about destinations, missions, or routes) is an important consideration. This force is task-organized for a safe transit from point A to point B in a cruising formation. A fleet in cruising formation operates in convoy with protective screens, taking efforts to avoid detection by enemy long-range surveillance, perhaps by satellite or open-ocean "tattletale" ships. The force relies on evasive steering to obscure its ultimate destination, all the while conducting a long-range surveillance for enemy searchers to provide sufficient time for evasion. Planning, rehearsal, and exercises are typical tasks in a cruising formation.

Once nearer to point B, where there might be more of a threat, the force should favor speed over efficiency (a characteristic of operational lift) and become even more dedicated to remaining un-located. Military deception (MILDEC) efforts would trump OPSEC. The force is now task-organized for the naval campaign and in one or more approach formations. Typical characteristics of approach formations are that some defensive screens might be placed at longer ranges from the main body, more longer-range searchers would be deployed away from the main force, and the entire fleet would begin to reconfigure relative to the threat axis. Logistics platforms might be detached to nearby bases to replenish in anticipation of an increase in demand. Ships would continuously zigzag for torpedo defense, perhaps even with evasive steering, if that supports the MILDEC effort.

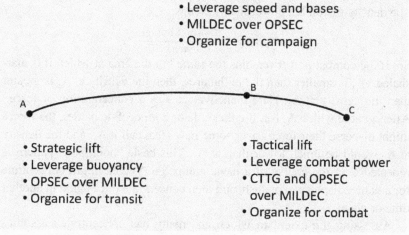

FIGURE 3.1 **CRUISING, APPROACH, AND ATTACK**

As the force nears point C, it should task-organize for combat in attack formations, with the primary focus of delivering combat power exactly where and when it is needed for the fight. This force is now practicing tactical lift (for example, placing weapons on delivery platforms like aircraft). Platforms should commence counter-targeting (CTTG) efforts (such as deploying decoys) and practice strict OPSEC. The force would configure assets for tactical search and surveillance as well as for delivering maximum salvos, providing mutual defense or defensive dispersal, as appropriate.

A force transitions from approach formations to attack formations because combat is expected. This particular transition is the most important aspect of operational-level maneuver at sea; it is the true lost art of naval maneuver. To envision how powerful naval maneuver can be, consider that naval platforms in approach formation might steam at 25 knots for up to a full day, covering as many as 600 nautical miles in that time. The area from which they might converge to conduct operations could be as large as $\pi(600)^2$ square nautical miles, which is more than 1.1 million square nautical miles (about the size of India). Twenty-four hours after converging, this force could be scattered once again over this entire area. This concept is graphically portrayed in figure 3.2.

Consider a force initially dispersed over some area, A_0. As the force is rearranged to attack an enemy at an advantageous time and place, there is necessarily an increase in the amount of combat power at that time and place. The density of combat power in any area is

$$\text{Density} = \frac{\text{Combat Power}}{\text{Area}}$$

So, if the combat power remains the same but the area at which it is marshaled, A_1, is smaller than the initial area, then the density at A_1 is greater than the density at A_0. Here maneuver creates a concentration of force.[5] After a battle within A_1 (or, if either side or both decline battle), the forces might disperse their forces over some new area, call it A_2, and the density at A_2 would be much lower than at A_1. This basic "hourglass" pattern is repeated over the course of a naval campaign. Forces might concentrate for a battle, disperse, replenish, and then concentrate once again in another time or place.

Assessing the extent to which an enemy has concentrated assumes enemy platforms have been detected or there is some level of intelligence

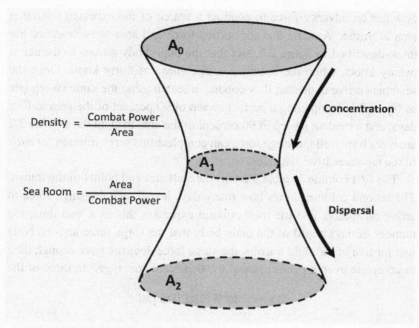

$$\text{Density} = \frac{\text{Combat Power}}{\text{Area}}$$

$$\text{Sea Room} = \frac{\text{Area}}{\text{Combat Power}}$$

FIGURE 3.2 **MANEUVERING FROM APPROACH TO ATTACK**

about enemy intentions. Absent sufficient detections or intelligence, it can be better to think of the problem as one of limiting sea room, which is defined as

$$\text{Sea Room} = \frac{\text{Area}}{\text{Combat Power}}$$

A force can reduce an enemy's sea room by conducting activities that an adversary would seek to avoid, such as overt, high-intensity searches, aggressive submarine attacks on surface platforms, or laying and declaring wide-area minefields. All of these efforts are intended to drive the enemy from where these tasks are being performed to more bounded regions elsewhere, in a naval version of "shaping the battle space."

LOGISTICS AND STRATEGIC MANEUVER

At the strategic level, recall the notional distances to theaters of interest in table 3.1. For most of the transit for these distances, a force will be in cruising formation, but suppose that as soon as the force leaves port, it detaches an advance force to conduct a search of the expected operating area in theater. Assume that the sortied force and area to be searched are those described in figure 2.6, and that the main body steams to theater at twenty knots, while the searchers surge ahead at thirty knots. Once the searchers arrive in theater, they conduct a search using the same sweep rate as figure 2.6, completing a perfect sweep of 90 percent of the area in four days, and a random sweep of 90 percent of the area in eight days. Table 3.2 analyzes how well the surge force can complete this surge mission for each of the representative distances.

The first column in table 3.2 lists the start and end points of the transit. The second column shows how many days it will take the surge force to arrive on station, and the third column expresses this as a lead time: the number of days ahead of the main body that the surge force arrives. Note that for five of the eight transits, the surge force does not have enough time to complete even a perfect sweep to 90 percent coverage.[6] In three of the

TABLE 3.2 **SURGE FORCE LEAD TIME**

	DAYS XSIT	DAYS LEAD	TOTAL DIST	FAS HITS
U.S. East Coast to Mediterranean Sea	6.0	3.0	4300	2
U.S. East Coast to Persian Gulf	11.7	5.8	8400	4
U.S. West Coast to Korea	7.4	3.7	5300	3
U.S. West Coast to Persian Gulf	15.3	7.6	11000	6
Hawaii to Korea	4.4	2.2	3200	1
Hawaii to PG	12.4	6.2	8900	4
Intratheater-1	1.4	0.7	1000	0
Intratheater-2	2.8	1.4	2000	1

Assumes main body speed of advance of 20 knots, surge force speed of 30 knots (notional destroyer at Flank Bell), fuel at sea (FAS) every ~3 days/2,000 nm, arriving on station fueled for mission

▨ = completes perfect sweep   ▦ = completes perfect and random sweeps

transits, a perfect sweep to 90 percent can be achieved (East Coast to Persian Gulf, West Coast to Persian Gulf, and Hawaii to Persian Gulf), but in only one can the random sweep reach the 90 percent level (West Coast to Persian Gulf). In other words, only the longest transit allows enough time for a sufficient random sweep, and none of the shortest transits allow enough time for a perfect sweep of the area. The surge speeds required for the shortest transits are currently unachievable by current hull and engine combinations, while the longest distances are so far that a slower speed would be sufficient.

Slower surge speeds may indeed be required. The last column shows how many times a thirty-knot destroyer would need fueling at sea during the surge. This ties maneuver to logistics at the strategic level since the logistics platforms must already be at sea and well ahead of the surge before the destroyers leave port. Alternatively, they must already be forward deployed or based somewhere along the transit to the theater of interest (requiring even more complicated strategic maneuvering).

LOGISTICS AND OPERATIONAL MANEUVER

A naval force maneuvering with the support of a base is conducting operational maneuver, otherwise it can conduct only tactical maneuvers—that is, for only a short while until fuel runs low and the force must withdraw.[7] Operational maneuver and logistics therefore go hand in hand, and the force is supported by what is called operational logistics. Operational logistics is more than simply providing the fuel to keep a force moving but also providing combat power (ammunition) and repair capacity to support recurring engagements. We can say a force so supported has operational naval power. A force with operational naval power cannot outrun or lose its base; otherwise it reverts to tactical naval power. It might fight one fight, but because it lacks replenishment must decline to fight another and withdraw.

The complementary nature of naval logistics and maneuver creates a crucial distinction between naval doctrine and ground and joint doctrine. Ground and joint doctrine talk about separate fires and maneuver. In the usual doctrinal sense, fires cover maneuvering elements, which, once in place, await the reposition of fires to cover a repositioning of the maneuver elements, and so on. Naval forces, by contrast, contain both fires and maneuver in the same elements, so they are always firing while maneuvering and maneuvering while firing. Moreover, a fundamental principle of ground force operational art is that large force elements are kept in an operational reserve, to be committed once a fight reaches a culminating point (where both sides are perhaps exhausted or stalled) to achieve a breakthrough at some place in the battle lines. But in contrast to ground forces (with forces in reserve), a naval operational reserve is literally *in* logistics.

Chapter 1 shows why salvos must always be maximized—and combatants themselves should therefore never be left in reserve but committed to every major fight. When depleted magazines or launchers are quickly refilled, it is as if a new force of naval combatants has arrived on scene for follow-on combat. For this to work, however, an operational reserve in logistics must be close enough to combatants, intact, and ready to support at the appropriate operational tempo. There is, then, a trade-space to manage. Logistics too close to the fight can be damaged in the fight, but logistics too far from the fight might not be quickly available for subsequent tactical actions during a high-tempo campaign. Balancing operational tempo, the proximity of logistics, and the combat power allocated to protecting base forces is a challenging task for fleet planners.

LESSONS FOR FLEET PLANNERS AND FLAG OFFICERS

While today's fleet is every bit as maneuverable and thirsty as Fiske's fighting machine, it enjoys a much richer and adaptable Fleet Train. Modern, sophisticated naval logistics systems have enabled a host of new maneuver options for cruising, approach, and attack formations. But these bring a complexity to planning and decision making that can quickly confound an otherwise seemingly perfect operational concept. The following lessons will assist fleet planners and flag officers in keeping the fleet moving and fighting throughout a naval campaign.

1. *Combat, Maneuver, and Logistics Should All Be Planned Together.* Too many plans de-emphasize operational maneuver and include logistics only after the smoke clears. Prudent planners will have thought through force concentration, salvo sizes, fuel burn rates, and dispersal plans well before a fight to ensure force regeneration is nearby and ready. In planning

for joint operations, senior staffs often devise a scheme of maneuver and then send it to logisticians to check for feasibility. In naval warfare, combat, maneuver, and logistics are so intertwined as to factor coequally in all aspects and all phases of planning.

2. *Logistics IS Naval Power*. All the elements of naval power—offensive combat power, defensive combat power, and staying power—are animated by and regenerated in a base. Without a base, all operations are tactical. This also means, however, that bases are significant vulnerabilities, and interruption of operational logistics—either by enemy action or by poor planning—is tantamount to combat damage incurred by combatant platforms in a fight. Of concern to modern planners should be the current inability for many advanced systems to reload and reconfigure magazines at sea.[8]

3. *Cruise, Approach, Attack, Regenerate, Approach, Attack*. Reintroduce the classic maneuver concepts into current plans. The hourglass is a useful image for thinking through a campaign of tactical engagements; artfully alternating concentration and dispersal is key to sound operational planning. Designing ways that make the ocean vast when it suits a plan and then compelling it to be crowded when advantageous is the most basic—yet most difficult—goal that a planning staff might achieve. Plans without these major maneuver and logistics elements will fail to follow up on a tactical win and are therefore subject to operational or strategic failure. Better logistics and maneuver win the battle of the second salvo.

4
CONTROL

It should be noted that, in practice, the exploitation of sea power is usually a combination of general slow stiflings with a few critical thrusts. These latter are frequently spectacular and draw our attention to the exclusion of the former, while point in fact the critical thrusts would not be critical were it not for the tedious and constant tightening of the screws that makes them possible.

—REAR ADM. J. C. WYLIE, USN[1]

Some parts of chapters 1, 2, and 3 might seem awash in mathematical specifics, but a full appreciation of the technicalities of salvos, searches, surveillance, logistics, and maneuver is crucial to understanding how they all come together in much broader, operational-level concept for fighting at sea. This chapter elevates the discussion to a higher, more coarse-scaled plane, but the principles are still concrete. The chapter begins by reviewing the most important ideas written in the last 150 years about operational competition at sea. It discusses how J. C. Wylie approached this topic when the U.S. Navy was at a doctrinal impasse and conceived of a new, general theory of naval operational art. The chapter then explains how the elemental activities described in the previous three chapters come together to compose the four main verbs of naval operational art—fleets *strike*, *scout*, *screen*, and *base*. The chapter addresses how these are the fleet commander's tools for controlling the pattern of tactical events in a naval campaign, either against a near-peer competitor or as part of a classic "superior fleet/inferior fleet" competition. The goal of this chapter is to explore Wylie's perspective on what modern navalists call "sea control" and to describe how fleet commanders can wield the four functions to achieve, sustain, and leverage control at sea for victory.

A BRIEF HISTORY OF SEA CONTROL

Our modern doctrinal term "sea control" has both a distinguished pedigree and a complex etymology. At first blush, it might seem as if a simple tautological definition could suffice—sea control is control at sea. But the main difficulty in fully explaining the term has less to do with describing what it provides (i.e., sea control) than it does in prescribing exactly what a fleet must do to obtain and maintain control (and in expressing what those who don't want to be controlled at sea must do to avoid such a state). Over the last 150 years or so a few great writers have contributed meaningfully to these ideas. A review of their insights shows how the evolution of the subject follows the evolution of naval combat itself.

The great maxim of naval warfare is that the prime objective of a fleet is destruction of an enemy's fleet. This is why early navalists, following Mahan, preferred the decisive engagement—a single, grand naval battle that could achieve this objective in one great clash. Sir Julian Corbett put the destructive role of a fleet in context. For him, victory at sea resulted in command of the sea, with which the surviving fleet could harry an enemy's economic lifelines, its lines of communications. Since fleets are quite expensive, his distinction between the means and the ends of naval warfare provided poorer nations with an alternative to the decisive fleet: these nations can seek to avoid fleet combat and attack seaborne communications directly. Corbett was describing the contrast between two classic approaches to naval warfare, *guerre d'escadre* (war of the squadrons) and *guerre de course* (war of the chase). The former employs the line of battle for a decisive engagement, and the latter disperses the fleet for commerce raiding. In the Age of Sail, a fleet wishing to forestall *guerre d'escadre* could dispatch commerce raiders to wherever the hunting was best (and safest), leaving the balance of their fleet in friendly harbors where they could remain safe under the guns of coastal fortifications. This resulted in what Corbett called a "curious paradox" of the "arrested offense": because an inferior competitor will refuse combat, a strong fleet is denied the use of its superior power and so must employ its ships in other operations, such as blockading, commerce protection, or their own *guerre de course* activities.[2]

The competition between superior fleets and their inferior counterparts evolved to an equilibrium that was unsatisfactory for both. Superior fleets could win command of the seas by forfeit, but they might not enjoy all its benefits: many of its ships had to remain in place to blockade the enemy fleet, which meant merchants under their flag might be at risk somewhere else. Similarly, ships on blockade duty cannot raid commerce or quarantine in other places.[3] Inferior fleets, for their part, were relegated to play the role of a "fleet-in-being" (that is, a fleet that occupies another fleet merely by constituting a threat, not by its actions). They were unable to break blockades to make their own *guerre de course* more decisive and were unwilling to take on the superior fleet directly. As a result, rather than vying for glory in the heroic decisive naval battle, fleets spent most of their efforts in what Corbett called "subsidiary operations of an ulterior character."

Bernard Brodie, in *Sea Power in the Machine Age*, argues that one of the biggest consequences of the shift from sail to steam was that it rendered the close blockade obsolete and upset this balance. In sailing days, unfavorable winds could keep a blockaded fleet from raising sail for weeks or even months, but a squadron powered by steam could attempt to break a blockade under any wind conditions. Steam propulsion led to the development of new types of anti-blockade platforms, especially after the invention of the steam-powered torpedo. The torpedo boat then became the favorite blockade breaker. Unable to engage these small, nimble vessels with their main battery and without another adequate defense, capital ships had to withdraw or suffer the sting of this lethal and asymmetric combatant. Large navies eventually developed their own compact, agile ships to combat the torpedo boats. In time, these "torpedo boat destroyers" became so effective that inferior fleets were driven to invest in submarine technology to regain an advantage.[4]

By the late nineteenth century, submarine (and mine) threats were a major part of an inferior fleet, creating a danger zone off the coast of its harbors. Technological improvements soon pushed these zones farther out to sea. In time, the submarine—once a blockade breaker—reversed roles to become a tool to engage a fleet directly.[5] By the start of World War I, *guerre d'escadre* and *guerre de course* had become intertwined, and naval warfare was on the verge of full-fledged stalemate: superior fleets were unlikely to meet an enemy at sea except under ideal fleet-on-fleet conditions, and inferior fleets—with no incentive to offer a fair fight—preferred to wear away a superior fleet's advantage in small engagements using what Churchill aptly termed "equalizing tactics." That the naval war in the North Sea unfolded as it did during World War I was exactly to script.

What happened outside of the North Sea, however, was not as anticipated. Ironically, the blockade breaker had also become the blockader.[6] Submarines emerged as the *guerre de course* warship of choice, even at extreme ranges from the coastline. Since this new threat could attack military as well as economic lines of communications, opposing fleets were prompted to invest in much more extensive antisubmarine forces. The result was such a proliferation of smaller combatants—historically, about twenty-five to thirty hunters are committed for every submarine perceived to be at sea—that a submarine force could also become a kind of invisible fleet-in-being (in this case, preoccupying a substantial part of an enemy's fleet, often without ever being seen).[7]

The end of World War I saw an unprecedented period of innovation and experimentation. Punctuated by the advent of carrier, seaplane, and lighter-than-air naval aviation, but including a host of Machine Age improvements (such as oil-fired boilers, larger fleet submarines, more reliable communications, and better ship and fire-control systems), larger navies of the world—and the U.S. Navy in particular—began to explore new ways to find their enemies at long range, employ complex screening forces, and strike further and with greater force than before. It remained extremely difficult for steam lines of battle to meet under favorable conditions—while avoiding equalizing tactics and protecting bases, sea borne resupply, and commerce—yet by World War II naval commanders were nonetheless preoccupied with creating a decisive engagement.[8] *Guerre d'escadre* remained the prime objective of every navalist, and the intellectual impasse of the superior/inferior fleet competition remained, even with radically new types of forces on each side.

World War II did not resolve the doctrinal tension between *guerre d'escadre* and *guerre de course*. After the war some pointed to the great turning point at Midway in the Pacific as evidence of the primacy of the decisive engagement (evolved, now, into long-range air engagements), after which the U.S. Navy was free to operate as a superior fleet against the Imperial Japanese Navy (IJN). Others pointed (contrariwise) to the U.S. antishipping campaign that sank 90 percent of enemy tonnage in the Pacific as the main downfall of the Japanese. Critics of this approach to naval supremacy noted the lack of a concerted IJN antisubmarine warfare (ASW) campaign, suggesting that if U.S. forces in the Pacific were subject to the kind of ASW techniques put to such good use by the Allies in the Atlantic, then the antishipping effort against Japan would have been far less decisive. Postwar naval leadership continued to debate these issues internally, but soon the competition between the services for a larger share of each other's roles and missions (and budgets) spurred a much more contentious public debate.

SEA "CONTROL" REDEFINED

J. C. Wylie observed the interservice roles and missions rivalry from his faculty position at the Naval War College and became convinced that the Navy was failing to provide adequate justification for its future mission set. He addressed this failure upon his return to Newport following an intervening operational tour, recommending a change to the college's research agenda. In his (probably Wylie-drafted) proposal to the Chief of Naval Operations for a new school of advanced study, the president of the Naval War College wrote,

> We are, as naval officers today, a breed of fine seamen, of able airmen, efficient administrators and of superb tacticians and technicians. But very few of us, until the forces of naked power stared the nation in the face, were able to reason with Congress or present our case convincingly to the people so that our own service should be saved from comparative oblivion. Our understanding and our exposition of the indispensable character of our profession and the undiminished and vital nature of Sea Power have been dangerously superficial and elementary.[9]

Wylie would administer the course; to develop the curriculum, he was given an opportunity to interview the nation's leading intellectuals from a broad range of disciplines. During this process he determined that any compelling rationale for a navy—and for the other services as well—must not merely claim historical self-evidence but should logically and indisputably follow from the premises of an overall theory of warfare. The theory that Wylie arrived upon was his theory of control.

Control has long been a key element of naval thought, flowing directly from Corbett's concept of command of the sea. For today's naval officer, sea control is the modernized notion. Substituting "control" for "command" in Corbett's *Some Principles of Maritime Strategy* will change neither his Edwardian idea nor its pertinence to its current Pentagonian cousin. Yet Corbett's treatment could not wholly satisfy Wylie's motive. Corbett wrote before the great air fleets, missile forces, highly mobile armies, and modern amphibious capabilities that precipitated the postwar roles and missions confusion. Corbett could claim his principles were self-evident because no other service at that time could do a navy's job, but for Wylie's theory to work, each service should be the logical choice to do the jobs they are given.

Corbett's kind of control might be called "jurisdictional" control. A superior force manages things in the area in which they are operating because of its superiority. It is the area and the objects in it that are under control. Wylie saw things very differently, describing a kind of "operative" control. In this sense, a successful commander controls the competition through a coarse understanding of how patterns might play out and by choosing actions that maintain advantage. A victorious commander doesn't necessarily command some patch of sea that is "under control" but controls the state of play between contestants.

Wylie was astute enough, however, to recognize that not all competitions are the same. Based on a seed that was planted by the renowned historian and strategist Dr. Herbert Rosinski, Wylie defined two main types of competitive approaches to warfare, sequential and cumulative strategies. A sequential strategy is "a series of discrete steps or actions, with each one of these series of actions growing naturally out of, and dependent on, the one that preceded it. The total pattern of all the discrete or separate actions makes up, serially, the entire sequence of the war."[10] Wylie illustrated this idea with four examples, the two great drives across the Pacific in World War II (MacArthur's and Nimitz's), the march on Germany from Normandy, and the Nazi foray into Russia. A cumulative strategy, by contrast, is "a type of warfare in which the entire pattern is made up of a collection of lesser actions, but these lesser or individual actions are not sequentially interdependent. Each individual one is no more than a single statistic, and isolated plus or minus, in arriving at the final result. . . . The thing that counts is the cumulative effect."[11] Wylie's exemplars for this type of strategy were the World War II U.S. submarine campaign in the Pacific and the Battle of the Atlantic.

While previous arguments about service roles and missions looked at the forces that might be allocated to different fights, Wylie's important contribution was to focus on the strategies with which these forces are applied. Each service might fight with either a sequential or cumulative strategy, and Wylie's insight was that some services have force-strategy combinations that are best for some roles and some missions, while other services are best constituted for others. He put it in simple terms: for very important reasons, sailors think like sailors, airmen think like airmen, and soldiers think like soldiers. These reasons have to do not just with how a service's forces are operated and apply combat power but also with how these forces interact with different environments (such as the sea) and the type of strategy (sequential or cumulative) that each service has found works best in practice. For example, sailors like sequential strategies when they plan to attack a large naval force in a decisive sea battle. In other cases like submarine campaigns, however, sailors prefer cumulative strategies. The forces for each fight might be similar (or even identical), but they are used in dramatically different ways.

But Wylie wanted to get beyond more than the roles and missions debate and understand more deeply than a mere description of the strategies and enumerating examples of each. From theory to practice, he sought a coherent framework with which commanders could deliberately plan to control their competitions at all levels of warfare, regardless of the type of strategy. For this he drew upon the mind of Dr. John von Neumann, the most influential of the big thinkers he interviewed. A famed polymath and child prodigy, von Neumann was a quantum physicist on the Manhattan Project and also a pioneer in the field of game theory. There can be little doubt that von Neumann inspired Wylie to view sequential and cumulative strategies by their game-theoretical counterparts, strictly determined and non–strictly determined games.[12]

An example of a strictly determined game is a two-person game like tic-tac-toe. It is possible to enumerate all the potential sequences that flow from an empty cross-hatch and a first move. Moreover, one need play only a few games before the dominant patterns of play emerge, resulting in a predictable strategy (that every child soon learns heavily favors the first mover).[13] An example of a non-strictly determined game is rock-paper-scissors. The outcomes in this game cannot be sequentially enumerated because each player "riffs" off the other, trying to deceive their opponent with feigned patterns, randomness, and second- and third-guessing. Although there are only three choices for each player in each round of play, there is no structurally dominant strategy and no first-mover advantage. Indeed, the players must by rule move simultaneously, but if one player signals their move too early, the second mover wins the round. In games of this type, there can be iterated play with variable payoffs; complicated, indirect feedback loops; or a high degree of uncertainty in measuring states and predicting outcomes.

Those familiar with both game theory and the joint planning process will recognize that the template for a sequentially phased campaign plan looks quite like a strictly determined game. This planning approach is in high contrast with, for example, the seven phases of the Battle of the Atlantic, an exceptionally non-strictly determined contest in which no clear path could be discerned from phase to phase and an ability to adapt quickly to correctly perceived enemy patterns was the mechanism of victory.[14]

From his experience in World War II, Wylie knew that it wasn't just sequential (*guerre d'escadre*) or cumulative (*guerre de course*) strategies by themselves that won the naval war but both of them working together. He saw that this was also true for joint warfare in all theaters, with the different services playing their unique parts, sometimes simply but always in a complex whole. This formed the core of his theory of control: both strategies work best together, an idea completely absent from modern joint doctrine. That strategies must be mixed at some higher level—that some parts of a plan must be simple and discernable but others must be complex and uncertain—led Wylie to his two main assumptions of war planning. The first is that the goal of war planning is to control the pattern of war. The second is that not only are the outcomes of war unpredictable, so are the patterns leading to those outcomes.

So how is one to plan? In Wylie's view, the product of planning is not a preordained dictatorial scheme blindly executed but an adaptive approach to controlling the state of play, informed as events unfold but nonetheless difficult for an enemy to perceive, interpret, and counter. This perspective informed his planning for uncertainty mantra: "The player who plans for only one strategy runs a great risk simply because his opponent soon detects . . . and counters it. The requirement is for a spectrum of strategies that are flexible and noncommittal . . . that by intent and design can be applied in unforeseen situations. Planning for uncertainty is not as dangerous as it might seem; there is, after all, some order in military affairs. But planning for certitude is the greatest of all military mistakes."[15]

Plans start as an abstraction in the mind of the commander. It is the job of the staff planner to render this abstraction into a concrete, actionable control mechanism. The adversary commander has a staff that is similarly trying to control the pattern of competition as their own commander perceives it. Just how a staff helps their commander gain and maintain control of the unfolding campaign—perhaps through continual adjustment and refinement as events occur, with feedback or feed-forward signals, or by manipulation of information—is the true essence of sound planning. Planners love to cite Dwight Eisenhower's dictum that "plans are worthless, but planning is indispensable," yet it is ironic to note how ill-suited the existing planning process is to adjusting on the fly once a plan has been rendered worthless. Wylie sought to build exactly this kind of adaptation into the thought processes of fleet commanders and their staffs.

SERVICE PLANNING WITH JOINT DOCTRINE

J. C. Wylie moved on from Newport and was soon elevated to flag rank, eventually capturing his ideas in a series of articles and his small book, *Military Strategy*. But the mechanisms of victory in World War II grew less relevant as the Cold War and nuclear competition dramatically changed the strategic calculus for all services. Intently focused on a new set of questions and no longer motivated by earlier concerns, the Naval War College moved on from Wylie's course. By 1987 the Goldwater–Nichols Act mandated and prescribed a greater cooperation between the services, and the Navy eventually adopted the canon of "jointness."[16] Discussions within the Navy of "why a sailor thinks like a sailor" gave way to questions about how a joint officer should think.

Jointness in practice requires joint doctrine, which became an early focus of joint force development. Perhaps in an attempt to adjudicate the differences between service doctrines, possibly to overcome service resistance to jointness, or maybe just to satisfy the greatest common factor in joint planning—the scheme of maneuver for large field armies—joint doctrine became a product almost wholly derived from existing Army doctrine. Service headquarters eventually reorganized around the Napoleonic Code, adopted sequential planning mechanisms, and reworked their own doctrine around the joint functions and joint operational art. Ironically, renewed interest in naval operational art came from the institutionalization of joint operational art, but by this time Wylie had been forgotten and naval operational art was reinvented from an Army template. Indeed, as it is presented today at the Naval War College, naval operational art *is* joint operational art, which is at its core Army operational art. It is as if Wylie and Fiske never existed. Today, a "joint sailor" is not someone who thinks like a sailor at all but one who thinks almost entirely like a 1980s-vintage Army planner.[17]

This is harsh criticism but not unwarranted. The services play their own unique roles within the context of a joint campaign. Universal, Army-derived joint language is twice insufficient: it is too generic for services' use in planning their idiosyncratic missions, and it fails to give the joint planner a complete understanding of how the unique parts fit into a complex whole. But the inadequacies are more profound. Given that each service also has generic tasks to perform (such as the joint function of intelligence), then both the unique and the generic contributions of a service must be represented with appropriate meaning and fidelity. This demands that joint language must be at once service-specific and joint-generic.

Instead of growing into a kind of military Esperanto, however, joint doctrine became a lingua franca. Every service except the Army has not only been forced to use the language of another service, but they have also begun the process of eliminating their own vernacular. So while there must be some common concepts of what each service does at the joint level (that is, we must have "upwardly compatible" joint language), by adopting Army-centric joint terms, we have lost the ability to describe and convey exactly what it is that fleets really do, even to ourselves (that is, joint language is not fully "downwardly compatible" for naval operations).

Consider the seven joint functions of command and control: information, intelligence, fires, movement, maneuver, protection, and sustainment. Each of these can be separately defined and understood in joint context, but when brought together for uniquely naval tasks (and navies almost *never* perform one without bringing some of the others together in a unique, naval way), the result is a dramatically different composite, best used with a sailor's skill on a sailor's special mission. But this joint language does not allow. It is as if the term "fire ax" did not exist, just things called "handles" and "heads," with no description of how together they are wielded to cut lines, stove in non-tight bulkheads, or drive damage control plugs with the butt ends.

The problem is less the fault of joint doctrine than it is the Navy's inability to express modern Navy doctrine clearly and in Navy language before developing the upward linkages to jointness. It is not too late to find a remedy, however, and not too difficult if one mines Fiske, Wylie, and Hughes both to describe the primal functions of a Navy and to bring them together in a Navy-centric operational art.

It was common in Fiske's day (and throughout the interwar period on into World War II) to discuss the composition and employment of striking, screening, and scouting forces. The base force—composed of logistics platforms, support services, administrative components, and even heavy lift for Marine Corps operations—was a major component of the interwar Navy. One can still discern the vestiges of these functions in today's fleets, but their lineage was interrupted. After World War II, the aircraft carrier became the focal point of fleet operations, and the trend toward "carrier battle group" doctrine had begun. Scouting and screening became massed around the preeminent strike platform, the "big deck carrier," and a special division of labor, the Composite Warfare Commander concept, blurred the lines between offense and defense. The bipolar competition of the Cold

War simplified and amplified this state of affairs (although NATO documents retained some of the classic Navy terms until about twenty years ago). But even these became hollow in the game of solitaire that constituted the 1990s' *From the Sea* post–Cold War operations.

Faced now with new threats and more uncertain high-end competition—particularly from an inferior fleet seeking superior status—we can look back to the classics to reframe our doctrine. This is the ulterior motive of the first chapters of this book. Chapter 1 describes the fundamental nature of combat power exchanges between fleets, which is, of course, the striking function. Chapter 2 presents the two methods by which fleets gain information about the activities of their adversary, search and surveillance. Their armed counterparts are the scouting and screening functions. Chapter 3 discusses the importance of logistics to mobility and force reconstitution, the operational level of naval warfare contribution of the basing function. Each of these main ideas is rooted in the classic naval thought of Corbett and Fiske, later conserved by Wylie and Hughes, and available to us now to reintroduce the primary functions of a fleet to Navy doctrine.

THE FUNCTIONS OF A FLEET

Current doctrine subsumes a navy's striking, screening, scouting, and basing tasks into a tactical carrier strike group. According to this doctrine, an operational-level fleet is created by amassing additional strike groups into an even larger composite force, the carrier strike force. Navies must abandon this simplistic notion to embrace the idea of operational-level striking, screening, scouting, and basing. Operational-level fleets—like those the size of the numbered fleets of the U.S. Navy—are best employed against enemy fleets in large, interacting bodies of striking forces, screening forces, scouting forces, and base forces. Before discussing how these come together in modern rendition of naval operational art, we define more concretely what each of these forces does at the operational level.

Striking forces deliver sufficient pulses of combat power to destroy an enemy fleet. A joint planner would think this definition too limiting. After all, isn't one of the main reasons one keeps a fleet for projecting power over an adversary's coastline to directly influence events ashore? That is perfectly true, but it is also not the main reason one builds a fleet. A fleet is raised to prevent another fleet from projecting power over *our* shores, so a fleet is first and foremost designed around a striking force that can defeat an opposing fleet, either to prevent power projection against our home or to permit it against our adversary's. What we do with striking capability—from carrier aircraft, land-attack cruise missiles, or amphibious lift—occurs with much greater effect after the enemy fleet is no longer. This runs counter to current pessimistic trends in naval thought that an inferior fleet's anti-access/area denial (A2/AD) capabilities are a permanent counter to a fleet-sized striking force. A2/AD efforts might compel a superior fleet to keep its distance but cannot compel it indefinitely. A2/AD forces cannot put to sea with enough force at great distance to track down and destroy the superior fleet—that is the job for another fleet.[18] Striking forces must be sustained by operational basing.

Scouting forces conduct armed search in support of decisive attacks against enemy striking or base forces. They also conduct armed search against enemy scouting forces to prevent them from locating friendly striking or base forces. When used in a cumulative operation, or when used against an inferior fleet without a decisive strike capability, they perform protracted armed search against enemy striking, scouting, or screening forces, often while distributed across a wide area. Scouting entails active search and reconnaissance and is usually an offensive, aggressive activity in which localization and destruction of enemy units is the objective. Operational-level commanders must allocate two types of resources to a scouting force: enough search capability to locate what they are looking for within operational timelines and enough firepower to both protect itself and conduct tactical strikes against dispersed enemy forces or other targets of opportunity. Scouting forces must be sustained by operational basing.

Screening forces conduct armed surveillance in defense of a main body (such as a striking force) or high-value units (such as a base force). They do this most effectively not in close proximity to the forces they protect (tactical screens are employed for this purpose) but by interposing themselves distant between enemy scouting or striking forces and the protected force. Screening forces use active or passive surveillance, usually in a defensive posture. Screening forces repel striking forces and destroy scouting forces, with an additional goal of preventing the main body from being located.

Indeed, success can be achieved if enemy striking or scouting forces never find the friendly screening force or main body. Screening forces are defeated either by penetration (through attrition) or by flanking. Screening forces must contain enough offensive combat power to conduct tactical strikes against dispersed enemy forces or other targets of opportunity. Screening forces must be sustained by operational basing.

Base forces regenerate striking, screening, and scouting forces and by doing so constitute an operational reserve. Because none of the other fleet functions can persist at the operational level without a base force, basing is the most important fleet function. Base forces are somewhat of an oddity in that they are the key to operational-level victory, yet they are the most fragile and vulnerable forces in the fleet. Indeed, the nearer that base forces get to the scene of the highest tempo operations, the quicker that their lethal power can regenerate the power of the fleet, yet this is exactly where they incur the greatest risk.

NAVAL OPERATIONAL ART

A list of functions, however, is not operational art. As is evident in the definitions above, all of the fleet functions are interdependent. The nature and character of their interdependencies—how they are brought together to mutually achieve a fleet commander's goals while thwarting an adversary from reaching theirs—is the design and logic of naval operational art. Wylie's objective of combining sequential and cumulative strategies is the ideal. But are only four main functions sufficient for designing a winning strategy for the complex competition he espoused? More to the point for fleet planners, are four interdependent forces substantially better than a single carrier battle force at achieving Wylie's goal?

As an entering argument, consider that two opposing carrier battle forces can interact in only one way, the classic clash of force and power. Reconstituting these same fleets into interdependent forces performing the four fleet functions results in about 4.3 billion different interactions.[19] Yet Wylie (and von Neumann) would say that we need something more than just a large universe of interactions to prevent our designs from being no more than a 4 × 4 version of tic-tac-toe.

That additive is information. The modern military planner is bombarded with concepts about information in warfare, most of which are contaminated by C4ISR dogma and self-justifying claims for information technology (IT) investment.[20] We are talking here not about new networks but about how information itself is used by decision makers in competition. Game theory very specifically and concretely describes the information conditions of competition: what players know and when and how they know it. In strictly determined games like tic-tac-toe, all the information about the board, the pieces, the rules, and the state of play are known by both players throughout the game. The information conditions are fully determined, with only two exceptions: the plans for winning that are stored in each player's mind. But so much information is known in these games (and, characteristically, so much structure exists) that a player can usually derive an adversary's plan during play, even in very complicated strictly determined games like chess. This is obviously the logic behind Wylie's admonition to avoid overly structured and prescribed plans. Non-strictly determined games are much more complex because the information conditions are indeterminate—information is usually obscured, manipulated, or garbled so that one or both players are unsure or incorrect about who knows what, when, and how they know it. This is the key difference between tic-tac-toe and rock-paper-scissors (and replicated at a grander scale as the difference between sequential and cumulative strategies).

Consider the information conditions inherent in operational-level naval warfare. Oceans are vast and fleets are adept at maneuvering large forces very quickly over great distances. The environmental conditions at sea can make search and surveillance very difficult tasks, and since modern naval ships are multimission machines, merely detecting a certain hull does not necessarily indicate what that hull's function might be, exactly what units of combat power are stored in its magazines, or what combat vehicles are carried on board. Moreover, a substantial component of a fleet can be obscured by the ocean's surface in submarines. Within this context, a fleet that operates as a single, large carrier battle force greatly simplifies information conditions for their adversary—detection of one hull is tantamount to detection of all—so their operational design cannot take further advantage of indeterminate information conditions. Moreover, platforms or task units found detached from the main force are correctly perceived as vulnerable to attack.

Contrast such a design with four somewhat smaller (but still substantial) forces, each conducting one of the four functions in coordination—but not in company—with the others. If part of one of these forces is detected, it precipitates more questions in the mind of an adversary than it answers. The enemy is left to wonder if what it detected belongs to a scouting force sent to locate their own main body for a follow-on strike, a screening force meant to intercept and attrite their own strike, a striking force closing for a decisive battle, or an enemy fleet train protected by escorts.

Now consider how a fleet commander might induce and exploit this kind of uncertainty against an enemy composed of a large composite carrier force. Perhaps what the enemy has detected is actually the friendly scouting force. What if a savvy fleet planner had already developed a scheme whereby a screening force lying in wait beyond the scouting force is ready to electronically mimic a striking force once the scouting force believes they are counterdetected. This would lead the enemy to presume the friendly scouting force to be a screening force, which they should seek to avoid—perhaps by flanking—to press an attack on what they assess to be the striking force (indeed, the relative positions of the perceived "screening" and "striking" forces would reinforce this mistaken perception). The enemy would thus be induced to strike at the operational screen, a first salvo battle one should welcome. This would have a dual, amplifying effect on the friendly fleet: the friendly scouting force, unmolested by the enemy's avoidance, can now close and trail the enemy's main body to support the striking force for the second salvo, which is itself more effective because the enemy has reduced its magazines during the first salvo.

What if the enemy correctly perceives the friendly scouting force? Perhaps our clever fleet planner has thought of this, too, and previously placed a second scouting force composed of submarines positioned so as to intercept an enemy as it attempts to avoid the first scouting force (which would have been operating in an excessively aggressive and overt manner designed to guarantee counterdetection). This gambit solves the scouting problem indirectly: instead of searching a wide area and putting its scouting force at risk, the friendly commander induces the enemy force to drive toward a waiting covert scouting force. Once the striking force is cued and attacks, both of these scouting forces can harry the enemy fleet as it retires.

This example shows but a glimpse of the broad range of options available to fleet planners who design their campaigns using the fleet functions instead of around a central battle force. Note that our fleet planner is able to employ both of these strategies in the same plan and execute either (or both) depending on how the adversary responds. There is, of course, no reason why a battle force can't be constituted if it appears that the enemy can be met and soundly defeated in a classic collision of pure power, but one should expect this to be the serendipitous exception, not the rule. Wylie's planning for uncertainty sets the conditions for an equally unfair fight, in which a friendly power play—the "spectacular" thrust—can be tremendously amplified by clever (often indirect) activities, such as those conducted by the screening and scouting forces in the previous example.

Some readers might challenge this approach. After all, hasn't there been an ages-old prohibition against splitting up one's fleet? Won't this invite defeat in detail? Why would you ever separate a battle force into smaller pieces? The quick and superficial response is that although the fleet might not be steaming together as one large composite, its parts are still cooperatively supporting each other. While this may be true, it misses the point: the main reason to fight using the four functions is to resolve the paradox of the arrested offense.

When a superior fleet remains massed, an inferior fleet should always decline battle. But if a superior fleet distributes its combat power, its superiority or inferiority can then be locally defined. The inferior fleet counts on this fact, hoping to create local superiority over an isolated component of a superior fleet, perhaps by creating a pattern of tactical engagements that brings sides together at a specific time and place to produce results favorable to the inferior fleet. Recall the "hourglass" from figure 3.2, which describes how a fleet might concentrate for combat and then disperse to reconstitute. The goal of the superior fleet is to concentrate from dispersed positions in some large area, A_0, into some smaller area, A_1, and then regain its sea room as it maneuvers again to a larger area, A_2. This scheme is replicated from figure 3.2 into figure 4.1. This, of course, is not in the inferior fleet's advantage. They would prefer to meet and engage some portion of the superior fleet under conditions that would make the superior fleet locally inferior, perhaps in region C of area B in figure 4.1. Here, a successful inferior fleet would have induced elements of the superior fleet into a battle they are neither prepared nor constituted for (their plan, of course, was to fight in company with a larger force at A_1). An inferior fleet should be led to believe that this possibility exists since that is one of the very few incentives for an inferior fleet to join battle. Knowing this fact, the superior fleet should develop a counter plan that foils this scheme. Inducing the inferior fleet to strike the screen, as in the previous example, is one such counter plan. The flexibility inherent in a functionally composed fleet not only makes it possible to draw out an inferior fleet, but it also uses the same motives in the lesser fleet, which allow it to be drawn out as key to a plan for its demise.

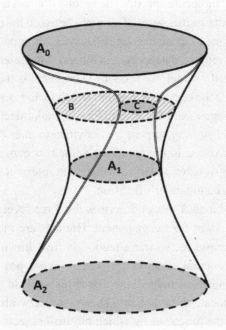

FIGURE 4.1 **CREATING LOCAL SUPERIORITY**

THE MOLECULE, THE BIT, AND THE STAFF

It should be evident to the reader that success in all of the examples above comes about by implementing Wylie's concept of control. Fleet plans should therefore focus on stratagems that create multiple ways to seize the initiative because the first mover has the best chance to control the state of competition. Initiatives are maintained by controlling the information conditions that ensue once the initiative is gained. While this has always been true, modern IT systems can be exploited to precipitate even more uncertainty and puzzlement from a fleet's first move.

Any networked, IT-enabled system, such as a modern military force, operates in three domains. The first and most basic is the physical domain. This is composed of platforms, projectiles, people, computers, satellites, fuel—anything made of molecules. Even the environment in which they move and transmit information is made up of molecules. Movement in this domain occurs at "molecule speed." The second domain is the information domain, which contains messages of all types between the physical objects, including collections of these messages (such as common operational pictures, intelligence reports, databases, and others). Movement in this domain occurs at "bit speed," which for modern IT systems is the speed of light. The third domain is the cognitive domain, which includes an understanding of compiled messages from the information domain, decisions about this understanding, and staffing to plan for activities to alter conditions in the physical domain. Action in the cognitive domain occurs at "staff speed," which is how long it takes a staff to collate and interpret information and then to facilitate a commander's decision.

The molecule-bit-staff model describes the three levels of competition that occur in a modern fleet engagement. Humans are most aware of the physical world around us, so our attention is first drawn to the physical domain. We think about force as physical: combat power delivered by ships, aircraft, or missiles. Indeed, the first thing we want to do in impending combat is to locate these objects. Those familiar with fleet operations are also aware of the processes by which physical objects are conveyed to decision makers: platforms are not presented merely as objects to observe but as potential indicators of an adversary's plan, constituting the rudiments of competition in the cognitive domain. It is not enough to note that information about physical objects is transformed into an approximation of the enemy's plan. Here again, information conditions dominate—who knows what, when, and how they know it is crucial to achieving a reliable correspondence between the physical and cognitive competitions. Competitors adept at obscuring, manipulating, or garbling information have a great advantage in information domain competition, and many of those techniques are known to a relatively small cadre of information warriors. But very few operators can masterfully exploit information conditions by manipulating all three domains of a fleet contest at once.

The speed mismatches between these domains alone create ample opportunities for inducing misperceptions in the mind of an adversary commander. Consider that fleets move at about twenty nautical miles per hour, and messages about their movements might move nearly instantaneously while staffs might take hours to correctly interpret the implications of these messages. It has become a bromide to say that victory comes from "turning inside" the decision cycle of our adversaries—what we should really aim to do is to exploit the internal synchronization inherent in our adversary's staff speed. A clever planner can do that by, for example, spanning important physical moves across an adversary's decision cycle so that discernable patterns appear incoherent from the adversary's point of view, perhaps requiring multiple staff cycles before any semblance of a plan emerges. If artfully accomplished, this technique could induce one or two cycles of error-prone forecasts that drive adversary behavior in precisely the wrong direction. These are the types of multidimensional feints and parries that can keep a friendly commander many steps ahead in a battle for control of the state of competition at the operational level, and they hint at the fundamental logic of what some might call operational art for cyber warfare.[21]

LESSONS FOR FLEET PLANNERS AND FLAG OFFICERS

The basic fleet functions of striking, scouting, screening, and basing are as relevant now as they were for Fiske (albeit through more modern implements and devices). The most important aspects of modern fleet competition are not necessarily the physical elements of these functions, nor are they the plans that drive their implementation. The mechanism of victory in fleet-level combat is the control a fleet commander has over the state of competition, which is derived from understanding and manipulating the information conditions in modern warfare. The following guidance should help fleet planners and flag officers develop the collective skill they will need to succeed at this tremendously complex, lethal game.

1. *Take Your Third Move First.* As Wylie conceived of it, planning for uncertainty entails developing a portfolio of moves and countermoves, not in an attempt to derive all the branches and sequels that a base plan might imply but rather to understand the important dynamics of competition. A clever first move does not usually give a good first-move payout but rather puts a competitor in the best position to get good payouts from future moves. Recognizing that our adversaries are clever in their own right and will think through the first couple moves and countermoves, a smart first move should set the conditions for and lead to a palette of third or fourth moves, each of which holds the adversary at greater risk. Planners should envision a pas de deux with their adversaries, seeking ways to wile them into increasingly disadvantageous dynamics as the dance continues (and it is best for them to think that they are "leading," unwittingly allowing their best decisions to draw them into even more disadvantage). For any of this to work, plans must always maintain the initiative—reactive responses are by definition moves in someone else's game.

2. *Give Your Adversary a Reason to Play.* The arrested offense is a case in which one participant declines to play the game chosen by its competitor. The only way out of this paradox is for an inferior opponent to believe they will profit from combat. It is vital to understand the conditions and motivations that invite your adversary to compete. Once you have discerned why, how, and perhaps where and when the enemy might join battle, it is the planner's job to exploit those drivers. Your plans are not likely to be successful if they depend on your adversary knowingly acting against their own self-interests. To put a stronger point on it: if this appears to be the case, you are probably playing the enemy's game instead of your own.

3. *Play Both Games at Once, in All Dimensions.* Wylie advocated playing complementary sequential and cumulative strategies. This advice implies that there will be determinant information conditions and simple structure in some parts of your plan and uncertainty and loose structure in others.

Mastery in naval operational art comes from using the uncertain and loose parts of your plan to mask the simplicity of your power play until it is too late for your competitor to do anything about it. Recognizing that large naval forces are not subtly employed, creating a hybrid of the complex and the simple can be achieved by extending the game to all three dimensions of fleet combat: the molecule, the bit, and the staff.

4. *Always Have Another Game to Play.* Consider it axiomatic that planning for uncertainty should always include a course of action for when things become too uncertain. Since a functionally composed fleet is highly adept at interdependent, distributed operations, when in doubt (or if a plan appears headed for failure), there are far worse things for the fleet to do than to disperse to fight again later. Competent planners would, of course, make this effort part of a larger plan, one that allows for another game to play. Think of dispersal not as the end moves in a failed game but as regaining sea room for a follow-on competition in which the initiative is restored and exploited on your terms and according to your next plan. Regardless of the state of play, however, one sure way to lose any of these games at great expense is to lose the base force, a condition to be avoided at all costs. Always play the base force protection game.

5. *This Is a Deadly Game.* For exposition, this chapter has used terms and concepts from game theory. The term "game" does not imply that these competitions are anything less than barbarous, lethal contests. Planners should devote special attention to the grim task of calculating the human costs of different moves. Whatever upside a portfolio of moves might suggest, risk and reward must still be calculated with the actuary's skill and the skeptic's realism, to include not just the outcome of salvo exchanges but also the performance of search and surveillance systems and the chances that an enemy isn't fooled when you think they are. These serious games are indeed deadly and costly, but they must be played to win.

5

FIGHTING FLEETS
IN THE ROBOTIC AGE

Some might think that this book has arrived just in time to be obsolete, as a new, nascent future of unmanned vehicles controlled by advanced networks and artificial intelligence render the main themes of this book irrelevant. To the contrary, this chapter shows how buoyancy, power, search, surveillance, movement, logistics, and control will all continue to operate in their same, uniquely naval ways in such a future. Just as striking, scouting, screening, and basing had a home in both the Machine Age and the Missile Age, so will they also be the means by which future fleets fight. The fundamental difference—a difference of degree, not of character—will be the extent to which future naval forces become even more controllable, versatile, adaptive, and survivable as these new technologies are perfected and embraced.

The key to developing the proper perspective on Robotics Age naval operational art is to understand these technological developments as being a step further along a continuum in the evolution of naval combat theory.

Hughes asserted that what makes the aircraft carrier the most powerful, flexible, and utilitarian naval platform was that it is a multistage system. The first stage, the hull, leverages the power of buoyancy to carry second-stage vehicles—aircraft—great distances very efficiently. These second-stage vehicles use the speed and maneuverability of air platforms to deploy the third stage—weapons (which are also carried efficiently great distances by the first stage). In the early Machine Age, when guns were the main offensive tool of the fleet, the predominant model for war at sea was, as the reader will recall from chapter 1, the continuous-fire model, representing a primitive two-stage system. Sophisticated manned air vehicles added an additional stage to evolve continuous fire into salvo fire. Aircraft were soon complemented by guided missiles (the unmanned vehicles of the Missile Age), filling the role of the third stage for large platforms like aircraft carriers and a second stage for smaller combatants. It is a valid logical progression to see the unmanned systems as further innovations within this multistage construct.

NEW LEVERAGE POINTS

On the most superficial level (although most programs have not progressed beyond this superficial level), unmanned vehicles are simply vehicles without passengers. More insightful combat theorists can recognize other, more operationally focused leverage points that have the potential to accrue substantial benefits in a naval fight. The first of these leverage points is flexibility, provided primarily by the addition of more stages. Consider an unmanned air vehicle (UAV) launched by a first-stage platform but controlled in flight by a second-stage manned aircraft. The UAV thus becomes a third-stage vehicle and might thereafter launch a fourth-stage missile. What is important is not just that another stage has been added but that since the second stage could just as well be a helicopter launched by a small combatant or a fixed-wing fighter launched from an aircraft carrier or large-deck amphibious ship, there is now the potential for tremendous flexibility throughout the fleet. Indeed, the third stage might have been launched from any platform in the fleet, even a submarine, or perhaps even a different second-stage platform. What this creates is naval power that is interchangeable between platforms, resulting in a fleet of first-stage vehicles—the hulls of the fleet—that now all have multimission and even capital ship potential, even if none of them have both.

Second, because a ship's combat power has been severed from the hull, combat power is not lost when a hull is lost. One thing that makes a naval multistage system so effective is that all the stages must be defeated for the system to be defeated. For the aircraft carrier, for example, it is not enough to sink the hull, since aircraft can redeploy to other decks or airfields. Nor is it enough to destroy all the aircraft, since more can be quickly supplied from other decks or airfields (in fact, providing a ready, nearby supply of planes and pilots was one of the primary roles of the escort carriers in World War II). Of course, if the third stage is defeated, the second stage returns to the first stage to rearm and reattack. The same is true of a future force with advanced robotics. Recent research using the salvo equations shows that when a distributed naval force meets a legacy naval force of identical strength, the distributed force dominates the exchange, due solely to the effects of severing the combat power from the hull.[1] Not only can combat power be preserved even when a hull is lost, the converse can occur as well: combat power can be replaced with interchangeable second- and third-stage platforms when the original complement is lost yet the hull survives.

Third, since a great deal of a fleet's distributed combat power might travel at airplane speed, operational speeds are now redefined. This effect was first explored in a series of wargames at the Chief of Naval Operations Strategic Studies Group in the late 1990s. The scenario included rudimentary UAVs transported by large special-purpose ships en route to an emerging regional incident. Hostilities seemed imminent, and with the UAV bulk transport platforms still almost 500 nm out, the UAVs could not arrive in time. But where the surface officers on the team were frustrated by the slow speed of the transport, the aviation officers saw opportunity: if the UAVs could be launched and sent forward to be controlled and sustained by the combatants already on forward patrol, then such a distant battle could be met with sufficient combat power in ample time. This early insight still holds true. If such a capability can be developed and refined for a future naval force, it would provide a transformational change in how fleet commanders and fleet planners view operational speed. Figure 5.1 shows the advantage that aircraft operational speeds have over hull-borne operational speeds in transporting combat power through an important area in the Pacific.

Such a capability is not so far-fetched and has ample precedent in rudimentary form. For example, World War II cruisers routinely launched and recovered fixed-wing manned aircraft, and it was common for Cold War destroyers and frigates to launch and recover turbojet target drones while on deployment. In addition, land-based maritime patrol and reconnaissance aircraft can air-drop torpedoes, which are similar in size and sophistication to many current unmanned undersea vehicles (UUVs), and the eleven-meter rigid-hull inflatable boat, used as the prototype for early unmanned surface vehicles (USVs), can be air-dropped as well.

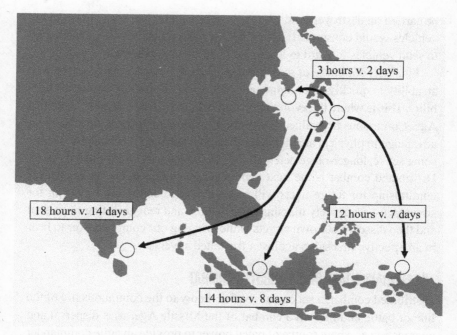

FIGURE 5.1 **FLEET OPERATIONAL SPEED REDEFINED**

So while combat power can be redeployed at aircraft speeds, it might nonetheless be sustained to the endurance levels of ship and submarine platforms. Indeed, the fifth leverage point, logistics, would also undergo significant changes when unmanned platforms are integrated to a future multistage system. In addition to the efficiencies already inherent in transporting these vehicles into theater by leveraging buoyancy, there are other logistical economies that can be invoked throughout the force. The most evident example is the ample aviation fuel that can be very compactly carried by smaller combatants (a much better use of weight and volume than actually carrying the vehicles). Less obvious efficiencies come from interchangeable sensor suites for late-stage vehicles. There is no need for separate antisubmarine UAVs, surface scouting UAVs, and airborne early-warning UAVs if a common vehicle can host different suites that do these jobs. With this level of modularity, the ships stationed forward might recover, reconfigure, and reuse the same platform to do all three jobs. Many modules can be carried on destroyers and frigates in substantially less space than unique vehicles would consume. It would be a very significant conceptual change to send vehicles forward to logistics rather than the other way around.

Finally, if our image of sea control is to control the pattern of competition, an ability to quickly reconfigure one's force is a profoundly powerful capability. This is where the evolution in combat theory leads us in the Robotics Age. Continuous fire valued throw-weight, armor, and speed to achieve an advantage in physical attrition over time, and salvo combat sought to overcome active, longer-range defenses with instantaneous pulses of lethal power. Distributed combat is the next generation in this lineage. The essence of admiralship for future fleets will be an ability to continuously morph for advantage—alternately massing, distributing, and reaggregating to present and then dissolve our own targets while bringing our combat power to bear in an effective first salvo against a frustrated adversary.

THE FUNDAMENTALS OF DISTRIBUTED COMBAT

Distributed combat, a successor combat theory to the continuous fire of the line of battle and the salvo combat of the Missile Age, uses dispersal and aggregation as a new source of naval power to provide an agile commander with many advantages. It will allow a fleet commander to disperse forces to dilute enemy offensive combat power among many potential high-value platforms but betray no obvious centers to attack. The fleet, meanwhile, would retain a tremendous economy of force, capable of massing both offensive and defensive combat power where needed. Because combat power is not directly linked to platform loss, and there would be fewer (if any) high-value hulls to attack, staying power would be very high throughout the force. Analogous to the multistage resiliency of the aircraft carrier, distributed combat theory maintains that the system is defeated only when all its stages and components are defeated. As a more complex system than just an aircraft carrier, the system is extended not just to more stages but to the networks and controls that keep them together. So it is not enough to defeat the stages. If, for example, an enemy tries to attack platforms, the fleet commander could order more distribution to rely on unmanned vehicles and the links between them. If an enemy focuses on the links, the fleet commander might rely more on hulls and local control of late-stage vehicles. If an enemy targets the late-stage vehicles, the fleet commander could disperse the hulls more widely and rely more on hulls and links. The key in distributed combat is to drive the pace and pattern of the competition in all these dimensions simultaneously to where it most benefits the force.

Distributed combat promises these advantages but comes with a steep cost: the decentralized command required for this new kind of control at sea will necessitate a cultural change at all levels. Unfortunately, this is exactly opposite to much of the doctrine and systems developed under network-centric warfare and its various progeny yet still in effect today. Even more dangerous is that there is an unstated and faulty paradox in the premise of network-centric warfare and similar concepts. If we "distribute our forces and mass our fires" as the concepts suggest, then only incompetent adversaries will mass against a distributed fleet. We would therefore spend tremendous resources and years of development for advanced networks, robotics, and artificial intelligence only, in the end, to fight our most incompetent adversaries. Or, more likely, incompetent adversaries could simply decline such a fight, and we would find ourselves confronted with the Robotics Age version of Corbett's arrested offense. It would be more prudent to consider our adversaries more clever and prepare for them to distribute their forces as well.

So we should expect distributed combat to be a contest between distributed forces. From this perspective, the enemy fleet is best viewed not as a set of targets but as a distributed collective operating in concert with a purpose. It is vital to realize that both distributed fleets are part of a larger system that also includes the operating environment. Here, though, Wylie is of considerable assistance: there will still be a pattern to control and a game to dominate. We should focus on devising new means to sense, measure, and model patterns of naval combat and become more expert in out-thinking an enemy fleet. In short, we must develop new tactics and, from those tactics, new ways to strike, scout, screen, and base at the operational level. We are overdue for this cultural change, and we will struggle in the Robotics Age, if not fail utterly, without it.

THE FUTURE FLEET AT SEA

What does a distributed force actually look like? The following generic operational vignette portrays how a forward-operating future naval force with the characteristics described in the previous paragraphs might be constituted, adaptively configured, and flexibly employed.[2] The scenario begins off the coast of Red, a country thousands of miles from the nearest Blue operating base. This country has long had an adversarial relationship with Blue and its allies, and Blue regularly deploys naval forces to the international waters off Red's shores. Blue currently has a small combatant and a submarine patrolling the seas in the vicinity of Red in a long-term effort to gain background intelligence on local conditions such as shipping and commercial air transportation patterns, seasonal variations on atmospheric and bathymetric measurements, bottom-mapping for potential mine warfare operations, and Red orders of battle. The Blue vessels conduct these intelligence operations by routinely deploying manned and unmanned air, surface, and subsurface vehicles; launching and recovering underwater arrays; and comparing locally acquired information with national intelligence products such as satellite imagery.

During the many months that these forces are deployed, Blue fleet planners have been deriving and cataloging the best rule sets for employing their distributed forces in this environment. Figure 5.2 shows these two vehicles on patrol (the submarine is below and left of the surface combatant). This figure does not portray the substantial fleet of small fishing boats, coastal merchants, and other private craft that would be found off any populated coastline. The commercial airspace and electronic spectrum would be just as cluttered. Based on all these patterns, and fully aware of the Red order of battle, Blue planners have established a threat axis, from which Red naval and air force craft would likely come in the event of hostilities.

Over the course of time, Red has become increasingly belligerent toward its neighbor, Purple, a country that Blue and its allies have agreed to defend. Blue's deployed assets have been ordered to increase their intelligence efforts to prepare for a potential deployment of additional Blue forces. The Blue vessels increase the scope of their air operations, establishing a defensive air patrol station (symbolized by the arrow-shaped aircraft icon between two vertical lines in figure 5.3) and an airborne early-warning station (the same symbol underscored by a horizontal figure-eight). After Blue receives intelligence on troubling Red ground force deployments, the Blue force is ordered to send unmanned vehicles into Red air and water space. The smaller submarine, ship, and air icons in figure 5.3 show the deployment

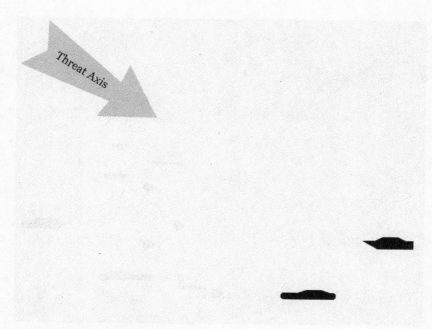

FIGURE 5.2 ROUTINE OPERATIONS

of unmanned air, surface, and subsurface surveillance assets. To keep Red guessing about Blue composition but also to most efficiently use available logistics and deck space, the Blue platforms increasingly share off-board assets, allowing them to be refueled or controlled by either of the hosts. This increases the on-station time of these vehicles while decreasing the susceptibility of the force to a successful attack on one of the vessels (since sinking one vessel does not destroy the unmanned craft deployed by the stricken vessel). Blue forces now constitute a core of deployed, networked combat power to which subsequent Blue forces can be connected. Blue forces have shifted their focus from a purely long-term intelligence mission to more near-term scouting and screening efforts to gain sea room for follow-on forces.

As the crisis escalates, Blue decides to immediately bolster its combat power by sending in more manned and unmanned off-board vehicles. Many of these vehicles are small and lightweight and can be deployed at aircraft speeds rather than ship speeds, either delivered by larger aircraft (for

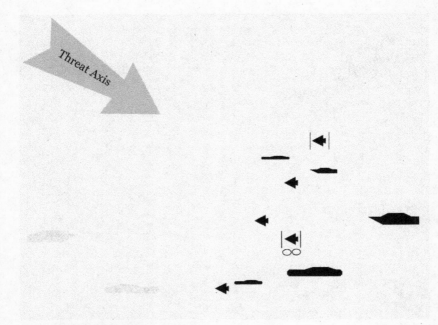

FIGURE 5.3 INCREASED OPERATIONAL TEMPO

unmanned surface or subsurface assets and some unmanned air vehicles) or under their own locomotion (for most unmanned aircraft). Since the in situ Blue vessels are built with a capacity to launch, recover, sustain, and control many more assets than they carry in their own hulls, they immediately assume control of the additional assets as they arrive. Some unmanned aircraft sent on their own are launched by manned surface combatants and submarines that are themselves speeding en route to the crisis. Figure 5.4 shows the arrival of additional assets.

The Blue units now have an increasingly complex problem to manage. The scope of surveillance and intelligence tasks continues to grow at the same time that local commanders must manage a growing collection of assets in an increasingly challenging competitive space. Blue has decided, therefore, to also deploy an airborne combat direction center (ABCDC, symbolized by the aircraft and acronym in figure 5.4), manned by a senior officer from the fleet commander's staff and a crew of tactical watchstanders. The senior officer in the ABCDC takes overall control of the Blue assets on scene and thereby frees the vessels' operators to focus on tactical, fine-scale tasks.

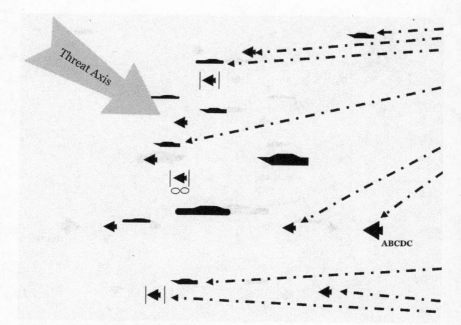

FIGURE 5.4 ADDITIONAL ASSETS ARRIVE BY AIR

Meanwhile, a main force of Blue vessels, including traditional striking and expeditionary forces, is traveling at best speed from their positions distributed throughout the theater to the crisis. The unmanned aircraft sent from this main force to the forward force are built with interchangeable mission modules that allow them to be configured for battlespace preparation missions (such as undersea and mine warfare). These vehicles are launched well in advance of the main force's arrival with the assumption that they can be reconfigured for their original host's use after the main body arrives.

The situation has deteriorated further as Blue receives intelligence that Red has sortied elements of its fleet to challenge the Blue naval presence in the area. Now that Blue's distributed screening force is well established, the on-site commander launches unmanned scouting sorties to begin tracking the Red fleet. These sorties are depicted by the curved lines emanating from the platforms in figure 5.5.

Meanwhile, the Blue main body continues its transit while the local assets maintain their distributed scouting, screening, and basing operations.

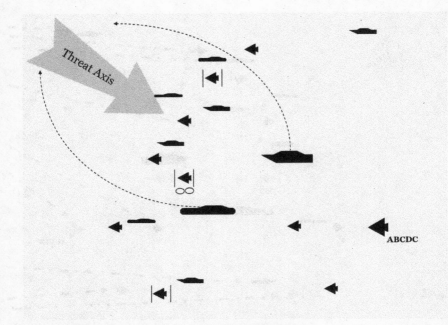

FIGURE 5.5 DISTRIBUTED SCOUTING AND SCREENING OPERATIONS

Unmanned assets continue to arrive by air transport or under their own power. Included in these are larger UAVs and air-delivered USVs specifically designed to beef up the surface strike capability of the forward platforms as well as air-delivered UUVs to enhance the antisubmarine screen. These will remain distributed from the local platforms, returning only to refuel, and then disperse. Figure 5.6 shows the arrival of additional platforms, including a package of strike UAVs.

As the larger forces grow closer, more Blue assets can be connected in a combat network, and the distributed scouting, screening, and striking capabilities are even more enhanced. Figure 5.7 shows the distributed networked force with even more multistage assets (including one more manned surface vessel and another ABCDC). As the main body of larger platforms sends more of its assets forward while the main force itself gets closer to Red, a very large component of combat power is now constituted forward, applied to distributed scouting, screening, and striking, while the main body starts building its own distributed scouting, screening, and striking network.

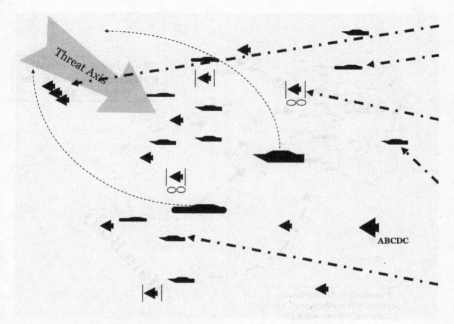

FIGURE 5.6 ADDITIONAL ASSETS ARRIVE

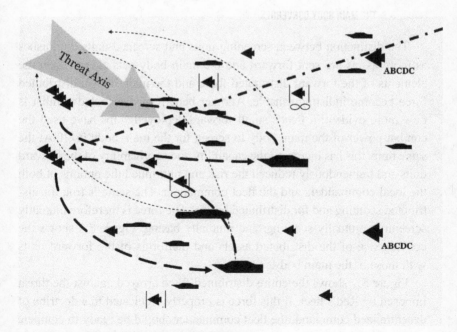

FIGURE 5.7 THE DISTRIBUTED FORCE IS STRENGTHENED

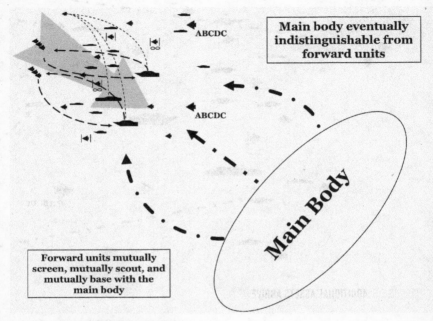

FIGURE 5.8 **THE MAIN BODY CONVERGES**

The distinction between screening units and screened units diminishes as more assets are sent forward and the main body gets closer. Soon the elements of the forward distributed force and the main body's distributed force become indistinguishable. Another benefit of distributed combat is now more evident: a fleet's small forward-deployed ships have used the combat power of the main body to screen for the main body itself. At the same time, this has increased the capability and survivability of the forward units and tremendously reduced the risk and multiplied the options of both the local commanders and the fleet commander. The same is true for distributed scouting and for distributed basing. The force is therefore mutually screening, mutually scouting, and mutually basing. Figure 5.8 shows the convergence of the distributed assets and platforms of the forward units with those of the main body.

Figure 5.9 shows the entire distributed force arrayed against the threat imposed by Red's fleet. If this force is properly inculcated in a doctrine of decentralized command, the fleet commander should be ready to compete

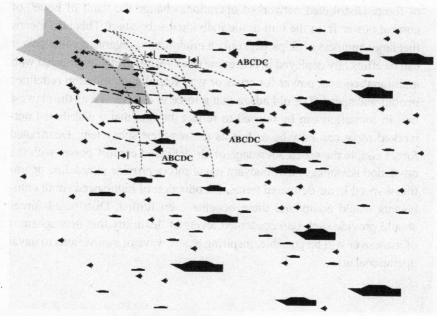

FIGURE 5.9 A FULLY CONSTITUTED DISTRIBUTED FORCE

in any dimension with the impending Red fleet, even if it is also distributed. The Blue force would have superior survivability because its assets are dispersed and operations are not crucially dependent upon a small number of high-value platforms; superior adaptability because combat power can be readily exchanged between air, surface, or subsurface controlling units; superior balance because distributed combat power can be massed for both offense and for defense; and superior sustainment in crisis because combat power can be sent forward to where sustainment is already deployed (in the hulls of the forward units).

There is a recurring debate in naval force structure analysis about whether it is better to buy a large number of small, single-purpose ships or invest in a much smaller number of very expensive multipurpose platforms. When combat power is interchangeable among the units of a distributed networked force, every platform in the force has the potential to be a capital, multimission ship. Having multimission potential fleet-wide means that a force can be highly reconfigurable and thereby achieve greater economy of force. Distributed networked operations change the "unit of issue" of combat power from the hull to the individual subsystem. This also means that large numbers of ships with only a minimum of organic combat power can be efficiently deployed in peacetime roles yet be rapidly augmented with additional combat power for crisis or war. Rapid augmentation redefines operational speed. The old adage that a force is only as fast as the slowest unit in formation can be revised to reflect the fact that a distributed networked force can now be as fast as the nimblest subsystem. Distributed forces couple the speed advantage of air-delivered combat power with the on-station advantages that buoyant naval forces provide to redefine operational speed in air-delivered terms. Introduction of high-speed small combatants would compound these benefits even further. Distributed forces should provide such unprecedented levels of flexibility that new schemes of maneuver will be possible, inspiring a new wave of innovations to naval operational art.

CONCLUSION

Wylie sought to define and analyze the mechanisms of advantage that, in his words, "give continuity and direction" to naval operations. Unsatisfied by the Mahanian approach (exposition of the elements of maritime strength) and dissatisfied by the Pentagonian approach (frequent recategorization of the various types of operations), he went looking for ways to understand how ideas transform the elements into operations. That *ideas* should be prominent seems lost on many modern navalists who are hyperfocused on technology, fleet size, and lists of what navies do. Wylie's concept of control hinges on winning a contest of ideas.

If ideas are the mechanisms of advantage for a navy, then why should naval thought be diluted into a generic joint concept? Some contend that this is the joint mandate. But jointness—a service's ability to work well with other services—does not necessarily compel all services to think alike. Hughes' *Fleet Tactics* contains an insightful appendix cataloging different versions of the principles of war. One version he expounds upon was conceived by Cdr. Chester W. Nimitz, written when the future Fleet Admiral was a Naval War College student in 1923. Nimitz starts by invoking "main and unchanging principles of warfare," each of which is sufficiently joint to properly belong in a current war college course on Joint Military Operations. But then he does something that would not make the grade today: he specifies in detail—with naval concepts and in naval terms—the implications these principles have for handling fleets. This is because high-level maxims such as the principles of war were viewed as empirical deductions about the character of warfare rather than officious dogma to be force-fed into service doctrine. Hughes notes that this perspective was common at the time: high-level doctrine set context, which was to be interpreted by planners and tacticians for the business at hand. He parallels this notion with another commonality within the interwar naval service. Nimitz and his peers understood not only the principles of naval warfare, but they also understood the processes of naval warfare as they were presented in simple, mathematical equations intended to likewise establish context for subsequent interpretation. The career officers of his generation shared this rich naval context for principles and process because it was established for them in the Golden Age of Tactical Thought by such thoughtful and practical leaders as Fiske.

Fleet commanders can win by ideas, but only if they and their staffs understand the high-level principles and processes of naval warfare and can translate that context into the kind of continuity and direction that prevails in a contest of ideas. Repeatedly achieving this in multiple dimensions—for the molecule, the bit, and the staff—will require tremendous intellectual change that fleet commanders and their staffs simply can't affect. Most of these chapters concluded with lessons and recommendations tailored for fleet commanders and their staffs. To build the context in which those lessons and recommendations bear fruit, the book itself now concludes with recommendations for how both the naval service as a community and naval professionals individually can lead dramatic intellectual change.

1. *Inaugurate a New Golden Age.* We need better ideas about how to fight, and we will be blind to them until we move our focus away from jointness and invest directly in elevating modern naval thought. It can be fairly argued that Cold War tactics and doctrine descended from World War II successes, which were the direct result of Golden Age ideas. The real and substantial Soviet threat was the forcing function that kept the focus on fleet combat. If the Warsaw Pact implosion didn't occur so soon after Goldwater–Nichols, then perhaps jointness might not have been so debilitating to naval thought. The coming information technology revolution amplified the effect: jointness and networking went hand-in-hand, both pushed hard by the communicators. One could say we lost command and control when it was fused to joint communications; it was about this time

that operational concepts became cartoons. The ubiquitous "OV-1," or high-level operational concept graphic, the entering argument for large-scale systems integration projects and a device borrowed from the software industry, began to appear in navy and joint briefings. Replete with "clouds" (representing major systems) and "lightning bolts" (signifying networking links), they became the hieroglyphics of operational thought. The shallowness of a Silicon Valley venture capital brief was sufficient to spur major investments in hardware and systems, and with them the promise that technology would trump tactics.

It is time to stop drawing pictures and invest in practical, durable concepts about the principles and processes of combat. Appendix B is just one example of the kind of thought investment required to bridge the chasm between an OV-1 on a PowerPoint slide and a fleet planner's dire need to confirm that there is enough combat power allocated to a force to execute a combat task with acceptable risk. Huddling up some Old Salts for a "rich dialogue," as the current doctrine recommends, is far from Golden Age quality research. The Naval War College is the natural home for this work, but if they had the capability, they would already have fixed the problem. Some of the necessary skills reside with the Naval Postgraduate School and Naval Academy faculty, but they are too far removed from the seagoing side of the problem to contribute mightily. Besides, serving officers and senior enlisted must be in the van—it is their problem to solve. It should be a priority, then, for the Navy's educational establishment to bring academics and uniformed faculty together to focus not just on the principles but also the processes unique to naval warfare. The goal would not be more dogma. A New Golden Age comes from establishing the right basic context so that all naval professionals—and all services for that matter—can have a meaningful intellectual awakening about how fleets fight and how to win in fleet combat. This awakening must be collective, not corporate, rising organically in the same way that the original Golden Age flowered—in our periodicals and in combat-focused war college research by uniformed officers. That we now have so many more ways to collaborate gives one hope, but it won't work unless we recognize how shallow we have become, and take steps now to establish the right context for interpreting the principles and processes of naval warfare into mechanisms of advantage in a contest of ideas.

2. *Play to Learn How to Win.* Once a viable context is established and ideas about how to fight a fleet begin to mature, the next useful step is to subject these ideas to a vigorous wargaming effort. Any textbook on wargaming will describe the purpose of wargames. Some are conducted as education, for example, to reinforce learning objectives in a war college course by immersing players in an operational scenario that features course content. Other games are developed to try out a new concept, technology, or force structure, a fairly common use in the Pentagon and think tanks. Others are conducted to develop teams. We will need all of these, but not as much as we will need games designed to train flag officers and their staffs how to gain and control the pattern of fleet-on-fleet combat against a highly capable, very clever adversary.

Chapter 4 discusses how mixing simple and complex stratagems and planning for uncertainty could translate a commander's abstract theory of victory into concrete, actionable control mechanisms. Such adaptive planning and decision making does not come naturally to many, and much of our recent, voluminous doctrine runs counter to this approach. This skill set can be developed through competitive, stressful play. While institutions like the Naval War College have a very robust gaming capability, most games need not be as costly and complicated as a major war college event. If we have been successful in developing the right context, including simple mathematical models of fleet combat processes, then we should be able to develop wardroom table-sized board games with enough detail to capture adaptive planning and decision making, which will contribute greatly to the growth of a New Golden Age out in the fleet as much as in our institutions. Indeed, during the old Golden Age, it was common for flag cabins to have similar "tactical tables" installed so that admirals and their staffs could develop and rehearse tactics for fleet combat. Repeatedly wargaming fleet plans should be a regular, routine part of fleet training at all levels. To do this it must be an organic capability in every flag mess, wardroom, and ready room.

3. *Take the New Golden Age to Sea.* Nothing teaches handling a fleet like actually handling a fleet. When New Golden Age ideas are sufficiently refined in wargaming, there can be no substitute for taking them to sea for realistic

fleet-on-fleet competition. There are many ways that modern shipboard combat systems and sensors can bring realism to simulated fleet combat, and these should certainly be exploited to their fullest. The real test of an adaptive plan, however, is what happens when things go off script—when ships fail to copy or comply with an order, when material casualties occur at the most inconvenient times, or when a wary enemy fails to take the bait from your trap. Once combat actually starts, it takes its own course: the plan is, quite literally, history. It is far better to rehearse fleet combat at full scale to understand and compensate for the manifold ways in which plans might go awry. A certain amount of robustness can be built in with abstract thought or a battery of wargames, but every sailor knows the unexpectedly unforgiving character of time at sea.

Some may say that it is much cheaper and easier to conduct large battle fleet training drills pierside with a combination of live play and constructive simulation. Such an event, however, is missing a critical aspect—it is precisely the cost and difficulty of fleet maneuvers that subject fleet commanders and their staffs to a higher level of stress and risk than they ever could reach in port. Presuming that senior naval leaders and their staffs will perform admirably in lethal combat without previous proof in a high-stakes crucible is exactly the folly of "expecting genius on demand" that Fiske cautioned against. We should want our senior flag officers and their staffs to be grizzled veterans of many demanding at-sea combat problems, playing friendly and enemy roles with equal fervency.

APPENDIX A
SALVO MODEL OF WARSHIPS IN MISSILE COMBAT USED TO EVALUATE THEIR STAYING POWER

BY WAYNE P. HUGHES JR.

NAVAL POSTGRADUATE SCHOOL, MONTEREY, CALIFORNIA[1]

A methodology is introduced with which to compare the military worth of warship capabilities. It is based on a simple salvo model for exploratory analysis of modem combat characteristics. The "fractional exchange ratio" is suggested as a robust way to compare equal-cost configurations of naval forces, because we cannot know in advance how and where the warships will fight. To aid in exposition, definitions of all terms are included in Appendix A. The methodology is illustrated with important conclusions from parametric analysis, among which are:

1. Unstable circumstances arise as the combat power of the forces grows relative to their survivability. (Stable means the persistence of victory by the side with the greater combat potential.)
2. Weak staying power is likely to be the root cause when instability is observed.
3. Staying power is the ship design element least affected by the particulars of a battle, including poor tactics.
4. Numerical superiority is the force attribute that is consistently most advantageous. For example, if A's unit striking power, staying power, and defensive power are all twice that of B, nevertheless B will achieve parity of outcome if it has twice as many units as A.

BALANCED WARSHIP DESIGN

Staying power, the ability of a ship to absorb hits and continue fighting, is a major attribute of warships. Developing a warship design in which offensive power, defensive power, and staying power are in balance according to some criterion, though ultimately a matter of judgment, can be enhanced by some transparent analysis employing simple combat equations. For example, the ability of a ship to absorb hits and continue fighting is a major attribute of warships. Developing ways and means to enhance staying power is a matter of detailed engineering design.

But the naval architect is faced with two dilemmas. First, if the history of combat at sea is any guide, when similar quantities of ordnance strike similar warships, the variance from the mean in the amount of damage is quite large (Humphrey [24, 25]). Second, even if one could predict with a high degree of accuracy the damage caused by, say, hits from Exocet missiles on a DDG-51, the difficult question would still remain: What is the military worth of staying power to the DDG-51 relative to its other combat attributes? For both reasons, the warship designer who knows how to toughen a ship does not know whether doing so will pay off in battle and be worth the cost.

Estimating the value of warship attributes, however, has always been of central importance to a navy. There was a time when the balance between warship firepower, staying power, speed, and endurance was debated publicly, energetically, and with the knowledge that

> You cannot have everything. If you attempt it, you will lose everything
> . . . On a given tonnage . . . there cannot be the highest speed, and the
> heaviest battery, and the thickest armor, and longest coal endurance
> (Mahan [28, p. 44]).

> A country can, or will, pay only so much for its war fleet. That amount
> of money means so much aggregate tonnage. How shall that tonnage be
> allotted? And especially how shall the total tonnage invested in armored
> ships be divided? Will you have a very few big ships, or more numerous
> medium ships? (Mahan [27, p. 37]).

The case for staying power in the form of armor was muted by the atomic bomb. We would have, we thought, one ship sunk with every hit;

survivability would have to come from other means. As the threat of nuclear war wanes, corresponding interest in staying power has not been reborn. The U.S. Navy has enjoyed the luxury of contributing to decisions on land while being itself relatively free from attacks from the land. But the sanctuary of the sea seems less secure today, along with the prospect of taking hits while fighting close against the littorals.

The problem now, as it was when Mahan wrote at the turn of the century, is to decide the proper mix of attributes in a modern warship. We see (in Appendix C) that the analysis then was framed by naval officers not merely as a single ship design question, but one of balance in a fighting formation, for there was a trade-off then, as there is now, between warship strength and number of ships. The methodology I propose is deceptively simple. It rests on the same premise that guided naval officers at the turn of the century: engineering detail adds no insight until the major attributes are settled by examining their military worth in a force-on-force context. But the simple salvo model introduced in Section III does not look like the force-on-force models developed then because combat processes with missiles are different from combat with guns. Nor does it look like other past and present force-on-force models for much the same reason (see Appendix D).

The purpose of this article is to offer a methodology to study modern surface combat in a form suitable to help compare the value of a modern surface warship's principal combat characteristics. We will emphasize staying power, which we think has been neglected. This neglect is expressed quantitatively in Hansen and Gray [17] and Hughes [23].

Although this article's central purpose is methodological, nevertheless there will be substantive conclusions. The conclusions are based on exercising the model with parametric inputs. It is hoped that the reader will want to conduct his own exploratory analysis with real, specific warship design characteristics.

DESIGN CRITERIA FOR EXPLORATORY ANALYSIS

We start with these premises:

- The best measure of a warship's productivity, or military worth, is its quantity of accurately delivered lethality, or ordnance, over the combat life of the warship.

- The best measure of naval force productivity is similar. It is the quantity of accurately delivered lethality over the combat life of a group of warships fighting in a concerted way.

Both measures of force effectiveness involve facts about the enemy that are inherently unknowable. A combat simulation, no matter how comprehensive and rich in detail, has little or no predictive power, because one does not know in advance what inputs to use. In such circumstances, some form of what has been called "exploratory modeling" (The RAND Corporation, e.g., Bankes [4]) is preferable. The modern way of analysis, including RAND's, is to use computer power in rather complicated simulations. The approach herein is the opposite. In the spirit of naval officer analysts like Chase [11], Fiske [13], Bemotti [8], and Baudry [6], we will aspire to the simplest mathematical model that captures the essential dynamics of force against force at sea. This approach is also in keeping with the highly utilitarian methods espoused by Morse and Kimball [30], [pp. 9–10, 77–80, 110–121], among others. For an introduction to the work of Chase and an explanation of why it was undiscovered for many years, see Appendix C.

Because a return to simplicity runs counter to a trend toward more and more complicated simulations, we take space here to describe the important conclusions in Beall [7]. Beall shows that a simple naval combat model can be validated from historical battles, but only if one knows and applies inputs that were observed in the battles after the fact. Besides actions by the enemy and damage effects that are unpredictable, other critical values that influenced the outcomes were

- Hit probabilities of ordnance delivered (unexpectedly low in many cases).
- When and how many warships in the force opened fire and for how long (rarely all at the same time).
- The distribution of fire among targets (despite extensive theoretical study and operational emphasis maldistribution of fire plagued naval tacticians in the heat of combat throughout the era of the battleship).
- Whether a force was surprised or otherwise placed at a tactical disadvantage by the enemy (the well-recognized tactical advantage of crossing the T was more often a consequence of accident than design).

The purpose of Beall's research was to assess the validity of two simple combat equations for continuous gunfire and torpedo salvos. His results show two contrasting things, both of which are nearly always true when applying naval combat models.

On one hand, when the appropriate combat model describes only a small number of essential features in an engagement, it will be validated by historical engagements *a posteriori*, whenever the small number of inputs correspond to those in the battle: namely, the ships that actually fought, the correct open and cease fire times of fighting units, the correct targeting of warships, the actual hit probabilities and the expected value damage of the ordnance. If one knows what happened, then one can reproduce the important features of the battle with a simple, but appropriate, model.

On the other hand, it is evident that if one does not know what happened he cannot reproduce a battle, even though he uses a model of any complexity and level of detail whatsoever. A model's dependable predictive power *a priori* is nil, because few of the vital inputs to the model can be known in advance.

The analytical approach of this study rests on two pillars. First, we are free to use a simple but appropriate exploratory model of modem naval salvo warfare that is sufficient to examine and compare the combat value of warship attributes. By appropriate is meant that a mere handful of essential phenomena are modeled in a fashion similar to the combat dynamics. Second, we must find a utilitarian way to compare attributes even though we cannot know in advance how and where the warships will fight or the competence of the tacticians who will employ them in combat.

THE SALVO MODEL OF MODERN MISSILE COMBAT

The basic salvo equation herein was first developed in Hughes [20] to show the tactical consequences if a warship had the striking power to destroy one, or even more than one, similar warship with a single salvo. The mathematical structure was applied to the aircraft carrier duels in the Pacific campaign of World War II. In 1942 an attack by one carrier airwing rather consistently resulted in one enemy carrier being put out of action. For a detailed discussion see Hughes "The Value of Warship Attributes" [22].

The possibility now exists that the striking power of a single unit armed with surface-to-surface antiship cruise missiles (ASCMs) may be strong enough to put several enemy units out of action, with profound tactical consequences. The salient result of this several-for-one assumption seems to be the creation of operational and mathematical instability. Hughes [20, Chap. 10] concludes that all classical concepts of force concentration are suspect when a several-for-one situation obtains. Victory through superior scouting is promoted in importance, and new tactics of dispersal and sequential engagement become attractive. But Chapter 10 also concludes that defensive power can reduce enemy striking power, in which case concentration for defense makes sense tactically.

Our analytical objective is to write a simple mathematical model with which to make exploratory computations that describes the offensive power of ships armed with ASCMs and the defensive power of ships defending against ASCMs. The model is intended to be descriptive in the way that Lanchester equations were descriptive of continuous fire. Exploratory calculations indicate that results are very parameter dependent, that is, case specific. In fact, case-by-case results vary so widely as to strongly suggest that detailed simulation will be vacuous until a clearer pattern of both the analytical and operational behavior of the various attributes is grasped first.

For example, when striking power (many well-aimed ASCMs) is strong relative to opposing defensive power (surface-to-air missiles, or SAMs, for instance), a first, unanswered salvo of ASCMs from an inferior force may be able to destroy a force that by all conventional measures, such as armament, displacement, and manning, is superior. This was not possible with guns because the combat power of a battleship was small relative to its staying power. It becomes possible when the combat power of a warship (its striking power minus the defensive power of the target) is large relative to its staying power.

MODEL ASSUMPTIONS
Definitions of terms are found in Appendix A.

1. The striking power of the attacker is the number of accurate (good) ASCMs launched.
2. Good ASCM shots are spread equally over all targets. A uniform distribution is not necessarily the best distribution. If each target's

defense extracts an equal number of accurate shots, the whole strike may be defeated, whereas an uneven distribution concentrated against only some targets would put at least those targets out of action. It is easy to compute the correct distribution when everything is known and control of fire is perfect; but knowledge and control were never sufficient in the past when targets were in plain view, and it is less likely that optimal distribution of fire will be achieved in the future. Thus, the assumption is as good as any for exploratory computations.

3. Counterfire from area and point defense systems of the targeted force eliminates, without leakers, all good shots until the force's defenses are saturated, after which all good shots will hit. Thus a subtractive process best describes the effect of counterfire. A simple model modification that includes penetration and hits by a fraction of the attacker ASCMs (leakers) is possible and in some circumstances advisable. The modification is employed in Hughes [23].

4. A warship's staying power is the number of standard sized or notional hits required to achieve a firepower kill, not to sink it. The choice is basic, because the amount of ordnance required to sink a ship is on the order of 2–4 times as much as is required to achieve a firepower kill. See Humphrey [24] and Hansen and Gray [17]. We take the tactical aim to be to put all enemy ships out of action so that none poses a threat, after which the helpless ships may be sunk without risk. Ships sunk is a measure of strategic success, in that a ship sunk cannot be repaired to become a threat later.

5. Hits on a target force will diminish its whole fighting strength linearly and proportionate to the remaining hits the target force can take before it is completely out of action.

6. Weapon range is sufficient on both sides. In other words, neither side has a weapon range and scouting advantage such that it can detect, track, and target the other while standing safely outside the range of the enemy's weapons.

7. Losses, ΔA and ΔB, are measured in warships put out of action.

8. For a discussion of assumptions as to the linearity of aggregate unit striking power and defensive power, see Appendix B.

THE MODEL

Force-on-force equations for combat work achieved by a single salvo at any time step are the basic salvo equations:

$$\Delta B = \frac{\alpha A - b_3 B}{b_1} \;,\;\; \Delta A = \frac{\beta B - a_3 A}{a_1} \quad (1)$$

where

A = number of units in force A.

B = number of units in force B.

α = number of well-aimed missiles fired by each A unit.

β = number of well-aimed missiles fired by each B unit.

a_1 = number of hits by B's missiles needed to put one A out of action.

b_1 = number of hits by A's missiles needed to put one B out of action.

a_3 = number of well-aimed missiles destroyed by each A.

b_3 = number of well-aimed missiles destroyed by each B.

ΔA = number of units in force A out of action from B's salvo.

ΔB = number of units in force B out of action from A's salvo.

THE MEASURE OF EFFECTIVENESS

To overcome the problem of the lack of *a priori* information about the employment in battle of a force, we offer as a suitable measure of comparative mission effectiveness what is sometimes called the fractional exchange ratio (FER). It compares the fraction of two equal-cost forces destroyed by the other under the supposition that they exchange salvos. Mathematically the ratio of fractional losses after A and B exchange salvos is:

$$FER = \frac{\Delta B / B}{\Delta A / A}.$$

When the FER is greater than one, side A has reduced B by a greater fraction than B has reduced A and so A has won in the sense that it will have surviving units when B is eliminated. When the FER is less than one, side B has the advantage of the exchange.

COMBAT POWER

We repeat Eq. (1):

$$\Delta B = \frac{\alpha A - b_3 B}{b_1} \;,\;\; \Delta A = \frac{\beta B - a_3 A}{a_1}.$$

The combat power, P_a or P_b, of a salvo is measured in hits that damage the target force. It is the numerator on the right of both equations: $P_a = \alpha A - b_3 B$ and $P_b = \beta B - a_3 A$. Combat power achieves combat work measured in hits. When divided by the number of hits a target can take before it is out of action, work on the enemy is measured in ships out of action.

FIGHTING STRENGTHS

Fighting strength is the term first used by F. W. Lanchester to describe the military worth of a force. For example, he said that under square-law conditions the fighting strength of A units each with individual hitting rates α is equal to αA^2. If the fighting strength of side A is greater than that of side B, then A will have survivors when B is annihilated.

The salvo equations show that necessarily, and paradoxically, a defender capability (defensive power) must be included. It may be deduced that the fighting strengths are such that:

If $a_1 \alpha A^2 - a_1 A b_3 B > b_1 \beta B^2 - b_1 B a_3 A$,
then A wins a salvo exchange.
If $b_1 \beta B^2 - b_1 B a_3 A > a_1 \alpha A^2 - a_1 A b_3 B$,
then B wins a salvo exchange. (2)

These equations hold when the first term on both sides of the inequality sign is larger than the second term. When the second term is larger than the first, the defense is too strong, no damage is done by the attacker, and zero (not a negative) loss results.

MODEL-BASED CONCLUSIONS

Inspection or trivial manipulation of Eqs. (1) and (2) leads to the following conclusions:

1. Missile combat is force-on-force so that we need to examine the fraction of each force that can be put out of action by a salvo:

$$\frac{\Delta B}{B} = \frac{\alpha A - b_3 B}{b_1 B} \quad , \quad \frac{\Delta A}{A} = \frac{\beta B - a_3 A}{a_1 A}. \tag{3}$$

2. Comparative fighting strengths of the two sides can be seen with a fractional exchange ratio (FER) by dividing one equation in (3) by the other:

$$FER = \frac{\Delta B/B}{\Delta A/A} = \frac{(\alpha A - b_3 B)(a_1 A)}{(\beta B - a_3 A)(b_1)}. \qquad (4)$$

When FER > 1 then A will have forces remaining when B is out of action, and when FER < 1 then B will have forces remaining.

3. Excess offensive and defensive power in the form of overkill now have a significant effect on results. The fractional exchange ratio must be used with caution when overkill exists, that is, when the combat power of either side results in more combat work than there are enemy units to accept it, or when negative combat power results because the defense of either side is strong enough to eliminate more than the number of good shots in an enemy strike. See the example in the following Discussion section.

4. From Eq. (4) it may be deduced that when each unit of A has twice the striking power, twice the defensive power and twice the staying power of each B, then B can still achieve parity (FER = 1) if its force is twice as numerous as A. This advantage of numerical superiority relative to the other attributes seems to hold over many if not all situations.

5. It is not true, however, that other linear combinations of A's attributes will also achieve FER = 1. If one doubles the staying power of each A, for example, then one cannot expect to be able to reduce defensive power to half its former value and retain parity. A determination of the relationship between staying power, striking power, and defensive power is the subject of Hughes [23].

DISCUSSION

Although further refinements to the salvo equations are possible and in some cases desirable, Eqs. (1)–(3) are the basic form for exploratory analysis.

Here is an example that illustrates the properties of the salvo equations, including the phenomenon of overkill. Consider two forces. Typical of modern American combatants, A's unit striking and defensive power are great but staying power is weak. B's force is more numerous but less capable, with its unit fighting value concentrated in its striking power.

Number of units	$A = 2$	$B = 6$
Staying power	$A_1 = 2$	$B_1 = 1$

Defensive power $a_3 = 16$ $b_3 = 1$
Striking power $\alpha = 24$ $\beta = 6$

With Eq. (4), first compute the FER:

$$FER = \frac{\Delta B / B}{\Delta A / A} = \frac{[(24 \times 2) - (1 \times 6)](2 \times 2)}{[(6 \times 6) - (16 \times 2)](1 \times 6)} = \frac{168}{24} = 7.$$

Without regard for overkill, side A has an overwhelming advantage.
Let us now use Eq. (3) and compute the salvo effects in an exchange:

$$\frac{\Delta B}{B} = \frac{48 - 6}{6} = 7.0, \quad \frac{\Delta A}{A} = \frac{36 - 32}{4} = 1.0.$$

A value of 7.0 indicates that A's combat power is sufficient to put all of B out of action seven times over with one salvo. B, though inferior, has enough combat power to put all of A out of action in spite of A's strong defensive power. In an exchange A's advantage in fighting strength is for naught. Of course, the weaker B is also out of action. What would it take for some of B to survive? B must amass a force seven times greater in overall combat potential; not until it has 42 ships would force B have any survivors.

From A's perspective we have demonstrated that despite great advantage in offensive and defensive power, its force cannot become involved in an exchange. The basic equations do not provide for an advantage in scouting (the ability to detect, track, and target the enemy) so as to get off an unanswered salvo. We will introduce the scouting factor as an embellishment in Section V. In modern naval combat, force A can only exploit its firepower advantage by teaming it with an advantage in scouting.

From B's perspective, an exchange of salvos takes out a force with far more fighting strength. Although this is good, B's is a suicidal task, comparable to an old-fashioned torpedo attack by a division of destroyers against battleships, or World War II torpedo bombers attacking aircraft carriers.

INSTABILITY OF MODERN FORCES IN SALVO WARFARE

The calculation also exhibits the property of instability when staying power is weak relative to combat power, that is to say, when the denominator of Eq. (1) is small compared to the numerator. If unit staying power, a_1 or b_1, cannot easily and affordably be added, then force staying power can only be increased and stability restored by increasing the quantity of A or B with units that have affordable attributes.

The unstable circumstance of very strong combat power on both sides relative to their staying power argues under all circumstances in favor of delivering unanswered strikes. First effective attack is achieved by out-scouting the enemy. Because scouting plays a crucial role, we will build it into the embellished model next.

The apparent instability and chaotic behavior evidenced in the simple salvo model imply the limited value of studies using specific scenarios and ship characteristics in any detail until the general nature of warship attributes and their interrelationships in modern combat is better understood. Studies tend to concentrate on the numerator, specifically, increases in single unit striking power or single unit counterfire, without sufficient regard for the denominator, specifically, unit staying power and numbers of units. To avoid putting too much capability in a single package of combat value, studies should carefully consider the relative value of greater numbers and staying power *vis-a-vis* offensive and defensive firepower, and do so in a force-on-force context.

SALVO EQUATION EMBELLISHMENT
TERMS FOR SCOUTING, DEFENSIVE READINESS, SOFTKILL, AND SKILL OR TRAINING

The basic salvo equations, (1) and (3), treat offense and defense as full up or zero. By the introduction of multipliers, σ_A and δ_A, on side A and sym-metrically for B, values of partial offensive and defensive effectiveness may be explored. Other terms such as a_4 for seduction, soft kill, and evasion are also incorporated. These terms enrich the analytical potential and flexibility of the model. They also complicate and confuse our basic understanding of the interrelationships, for we increase the number of parametric attributes from 8 to as many as 14.

ASSUMPTIONS

1. Scouting effectiveness, σ_A or σ_B takes values between 0 and 1 that measure the extent to which striking power is diminished due to less-than-perfect targeting and distribution of fire against the target force.

2. Similarly, defender alertness, or readiness, δ_A or δ_B, takes values between 0 and 1 that measure the extent to which counterfire is diminished due to less-than-perfect readiness or fire control designation to destroy the missiles of an enemy attack.

3. Seduction chaff causes otherwise accurate shots to miss after counterfire has failed. We assume that it draws off all such good enemy shots with the same probability, a_4 or b_4 against each. The model also assumes that the probability does not change as the number of defenders employing it are reduced. Evasion, by low observability or avoidance of a weapon such as a torpedo, is treated mathematically in the same way as seduction chaff.

4. Distraction chaff draws off shots before counterfire, thereby reducing the number of accurate shots that must be destroyed by counterfire. It is given a fixed probability of distracting each enemy shot. Designated ρ_A or ρ_B, it is a multiplier between 0 and 1 applied to βB and αA, respectively.

5. A force will fail to reach its full combat potential in part due to inadequate training, organization or motivation. The degree to which a firing unit or target unit thereby fails to achieve its potential is a skillfulness, or training, multiplier, τ_A or τ_B, that takes values between 0 and 1 and is applied where appropriate. Hatzopoulis [18] is the first naval officer to think of this straightforward way to reflect human factors in naval force-on-force equations.

FORCE-ON-FORCE EQUATIONS

Let $\alpha' = \sigma_A \tau_A \rho_B \alpha$ be the fighting power in hits of an attacking unit of side A modified for scouting and training deficiencies and the effect of defender B's distraction chaff.

Let $\beta' = \sigma_B \tau_B \rho_A \beta$ be the fighting power in hits of an attacking unit of side B modified for scouting and training deficiencies and the effect of defender A's distraction chaff.

Let $b'_3 = \delta_B \tau_B b_3$ be the hits denied to A by defender counterfire of B, degraded for defender alertness and training deficiencies.

Let $a'_3 = \delta_A \tau_A a_3$ be the hits denied to B by defender counterfire of A, degraded for defender alertness and training deficiencies.

Then the embellished force-on-force equations, including seduction and evasion terms, are

$$\Delta B = \frac{(\alpha'A - b_3'B)b_4}{b_1} \quad , \quad \Delta A = \frac{(\beta'B - a_3'A)a_4}{a_1}. \quad (5)$$

MODEL-BASED CONCLUSIONS

1. Both striking power, α' or β', and defensive power, a_3' or b_3', depend on good scouting. Concentration of forces (the number of participating units, A or B) depends on effective leadership and tactics. But force staying power (a_1A) is in the main a design attribute that is independent of the degree of success in scouting and tactical concentration.

2. For exploratory analysis, the whole of scouting's effect on a combat outcome can be reduced to four multipliers, σ_A, σ_B, δ_B, and δ_B, that take values between 0 and 1 to diminish each side's striking power and counterfire.

3. Similarly, the effects of any and all training deficiencies are not difficult to incorporate. This seems useful to know, however constrained we are in quantifying τ for ourselves and the enemy.

DISCUSSION

As to explicit representations of own and enemy scouting, they are very difficult to express quantitatively in the absence of combat specifics. The mathematics of scouting effectiveness is well developed and robust; the principal failure is in marrying the scouting and shooting process into a single system of evaluation. In sharp contrast, the mathematics—indeed, the entire art—of diminishing enemy scouting capability is weak and undeveloped.

Nevertheless the equations tell us *how* and where to introduce scouting's effect. It seems particularly important to include it as a factor that degrades defensive power. Many things, including too-strict EMCON, enemy deception and stealth, and confusion over whether all enemy units have been detected and targeted, can cause a surprise attack, which in salvo warfare is likely to be fatal. We do not know in most exploratory analyses what numbers to assign to σ and δ. The vital point, which is that success in modern salvo warfare centers on superior scouting, has already been made.

It is also worth reaffirming that the best way to soften the consequences of scouting weakness is to increase the value of the salvo equations' denominator with either greater numbers of units or greater staying power per unit, or both.

Deficiencies in combat skill—what we have called training—are also placed in combat context with the salvo equation. There is a continuing undercurrent of emotional appeals for the enhancement of organizational, doctrinal, motivational, and other human factors without specifying where and how the factors affect combat results. The placement of τ in the equations is apparently the necessary and sufficient way to do this. It is not difficult in the framework of the salvo equation to compare the value of money spent on people versus the value of money spent on their machines. Most importantly, the equations declare that there is no such thing as a training bonus or synergism. Our studies almost always assume the skillful employment of sensors and weapons when we measure their designed combat potential or estimate their combat power. When human operators enter combat, they seldom achieve the full potential of their machines. The most we can hope for is that they come close to doing so.

CONCLUSIONS

1. *Terminology.* For clear communication, unambiguous definitions of naval combat terms should be agreed upon within the U.S. Navy and adopted. In particular, combat power and survivability take on a variety of meanings. Definitions are set forth in Appendix A.

2. *Own Attributes.* The key attributes that bear heavily on success in modern surface and air-surface naval combat are:

- Striking power
- Staying power
- Counterfire (defensive firepower)
- Scouting (detection and targeting) effectiveness
- Soft-kill counteractions
- Defensive readiness
- Training, organization, doctrine, and motivation (resulting in skill and referred to collectively herein as "training").

No attribute may be neglected in warship design, peacetime drills, or combat operations. While this conclusion is derived from an examination of the phenomenon of modern missile combat rather than from manipulation of the salvo equations, relationships between attributes may be grasped from the equations, permitting the study of any element's contribution alone or in combination.

3. *Enemy Attributes and the FER.* It is a fact of combat that the attributes of the enemy in battle are coequal determinants of its outcome. That the enemy's numbers and quality are a vital ingredient in ship design that cannot be known during warship configuration has, to say the least, complicated the design problem. The fractional exchange ratio (FER) is advanced as a robust way to compare warship attributes in the absence of knowledge about the circumstances in which a warship will fight, including the attributes of the enemy.

4. *C2.* Command and control do not appear in the equation because they affect many of the terms on both sides:

- Scouting effectiveness
- Striking power generated
- Counteractions generated against enemy striking power
- State of training
- Even numbers of engaged units, A or B, are affected, because it is a primary command responsibility to bring all forces to bear in a battle while at the same time inhibiting the enemy's ability to do so.

5. *Staying Power Robustness.* Ship staying power is uniquely the ship design element least affected by the particulars of a battle, including poor tactics. Staying power's inherent robustness suggests that it should be treated with great respect; and specifically with greater respect in U.S. Navy ship designs, which have little staying power relative to other attributes such as striking power and defensive hardkill and softkill power.

6. *Advantage of Numbers.* The attribute that is the most consistently advantageous in force-on-force engagements is the number of combat units. For example, if A's unit striking power, staying power, and defensive power are all twice that of each B, then force B is still able to achieve parity

of outcome if it has twice as many units as A. The special combat advantage of numbers seems to apply under a very wide set of circumstances.

7. *Quantity and Quality.* Because increasing the number of warships is costly, as there are usually economies of scale from building capability into fewer, larger ships, and further because there is such a thing as minimum feasible size, for example, of aircraft carriers and AEGIS-type combatants, an abstract preference for quantity may be impractical. But three things suggested by the combat model are so important that they ought to be further tested:

- When small warships are capable of delivering large salvos, unstable, hazardous conditions are much more likely to occur than was ever the case in the big gun era or even the era when carrier aircraft attacked with bombs and torpedoes. This leads to new and different preferences for the various attributes, some of which are pointed out in these conclusions. The goal of balance in warship design takes on added significance in the missile area.
- Fleets weak in staying power relative to their combat power are in an unstable condition. They are subject to destruction and defeat at the same time their ordnance is delivered. Such fleets must operate in a highly risk-averse mode, as if tactically paranoid. Conclusion 8 specifies unstable conditions.
- Although it has always been tactically desirable to attack without corresponding return fire, now even a superior force must, in unstable circumstances, attack decisively first to win without severe losses. The salvo equations show why this is so and, quantitatively, the consequences of failure to prevent an attack by a weaker opponent. Also see conclusion 9.

8. *Tactical Instability.* As the combat power of either force grows relative to the staying power of that force, the risk of unstable circumstances grows with it. The condition of instability is characterized by opportunities for the inferior side to win or do proportionately more severe damage to the superior side in an exchange, or to defeat it with a surprise attack.

9. *Scouting's Importance.* The potential value of missiles that outrange the enemy will receive even greater weight when the consequences of

tactical instability are fully understood. But the potential of longer-range weapons cannot be realized without good scouting to detect and track the enemy. Whether or not one side has a range advantage, success in delivering a decisive missile salvo depends more than anything else on its superior scouting. Success in forestalling the enemy's strike depends on interfering with his scouting, and the C2 which marries together his sensors and weapons.

10. *Warship Design Goal.* Maximum fighting strength (i.e., hits achieved during a combat lifetime) is the proper warship design goal. Experimentation with all parameters except numbers of forces shows no consistent preference in favor of striking power, counterfire, or staying power to achieve the goal. Preference seems to depend on varying relationships between the values on both sides that are particular to each sea battle. The instability that is seen under many circumstances implies a limited value of studies that use specific scenarios and detailed ship characteristics, until the general nature of warship attributes and their interrelationships is better understood. Procurement and design studies tend to concentrate only on fleet combat power, or even more narrowly on single-unit striking power and single-unit counterfire, without sufficient regard for other attributes. In particular, this study indicates the need for attention to whole-force staying power, which is the product of unit staying power multiplied by the number of units engaged. To achieve balance and avoid building an unsustainable amount of offensive and defensive firepower into individual warships, detailed studies must be done in a force-on-force context in which the relative worth of offensive and defensive power is compared with the worth of greater numbers and staying power.

11. *About Staying Power.*

- The salvo equations do not embrace undersea warfare. It is important to realize that design features suggested by the salvo equations will understate the value of staying power, which when present contributes uniquely to survival against torpedoes and mines as well as shells and missiles.
- In littoral operations the effectiveness of defensive systems, a_3 and a_4, will be curtailed because of short response time, in which case survival and the ability to fulfill a mission will depend more heavily on staying power.

APPENDIX A. DEFINITIONS

Definitions both bold and centered[2] are followed by mathematical symbols that appear in the models of combat processes represented in the study.

COMBAT UNIT

1. A ship or aircraft capable of delivering firepower.
2. An actual or notional warship/aircraft type comprising a homogeneous force.
3. A standard or benchmark unit in a heterogeneous force.

COMBAT FORCE

A group of COMBAT UNITS that operate and fight in concert.

FORCE STRENGTH. A, B.

1. The number of UNITS in a homogeneous COMBAT FORCE on sides A or B, designated A or B, respectively.
2. The total value of a heterogeneous FORCE is a weighted sum of the individual UNIT values measured against a standard unit, for example, an FFG-7. The FORCE STRENGTH is A or B measured in standard unit values.

SHOT

1. A single unit of ordnance, for example, shell, torpedo, missile.
2. A notional unit of ordnance in a homogeneous force, for example, an HC-type 8-inch shell, a Mark XII 21-inch torpedo, or a Harpoon missile.
3. A standard or benchmark unit of ordnance in a heterogeneous force.

HIT

Verb: To deliver an accurate SHOT to a UNIT.

Noun: 1. A SHOT that inflicts damage proportionate to $1/a_1$ or $1/b_1$ of a target UNIT's STAYING POWER. 2. The fundamental unit of measurement of FIREPOWER, FIGHTING POWER, STRIKING POWER, and COMBAT POWER.

SEEN TARGET

An enemy COMBAT UNIT that is detected, tracked, and targetable. By targetable is meant a UNIT at which a SHOT may be fired with a utilitarian ACCURACY OF FIRE.

ACCURATE SHOT, OR GOOD SHOT

A SHOT that is so well aimed that it will HIT a SEEN TARGET, absent actions by the target to avoid it. An ACCURATE, or GOOD, SHOT must in some cases be defined with respect to specific aspect and motion of the target.

ACCURACY OF FIRE. π_A, π_B.

The probability that a SHOT fired against a target will be an ACCURATE SHOT.

COMBAT KILL, OR MISSION KILL

Verb: To put out of action (OOA); to render impotent for the duration of an engagement.

Noun: The state of a COMBAT UNIT that is out of action and rendered harmless, not necessarily sunk, but with no COMBAT POWER remaining. (COMBAT POWER is defined in the following.)

OFFENSIVE POWER

A casual expression of FIREPOWER, FIGHTING POWER, STRIKING POWER, or COMBAT POWER as appropriate to the circumstances.

OVERKILL

A casual word for the excess or surplus of OFFENSIVE POWER in hits on targets that exceed the number necessary for COMBAT KILL. OVER-KILL is a valuable, but not always desirable, margin to cover errors, mis-calculations or chance. It is also a measure of damage beyond COMBAT KILL toward a sinking.

FIREPOWER. Unit: a_2, b_2. Force: a_2A, b_2B.
1. Of a COMBAT UNIT, the rate at which SHOTS are fired by the UNIT, whether ACCURATE or not.
   a. Per unit of time for a stream of SHOTS, called continuous fire.

b. Per salvo for a pulse or bundle of SHOTS tightly spaced in time relative to the interval between pulses (called salvo fire).

2. Of a FORCE, the rate at which SHOTS are fired by all UNITS.
   a. Per unit time for continuous fire.
   b. Per tightly spaced pulse for salvo fire.

Firepower is frequently but unwisely used as a basis for comparison with other attributes.

FIGHTING POWER, or STRIKING POWER.
Unit: α, β. Force: αA, βB

1. Of a COMBAT UNIT, the number of ACCURATE SHOTS fired by it.
   a. Per period of time for continuous fire.
   b. Per tightly spaced pulse for salvo fire.
2. Of a FORCE, the number of ACCURATE SHOTS fired by all UNITS.
   a. Per period of time for continuous fire.
   b. Per tightly spaced pulse for salvo fire.

FIGHTING POWER is FIREPOWER diminished for ACCURACY OF FIRE. Also called STRIKING POWER for carrier air or missile strike.

STAYING POWER. Unit: a_1, b_1. Force: a_1A, b_1B.
The number of HITS that can be absorbed by a UNIT or FORCE before COMBAT POWER (equivalently, FIREPOWER and FIGHTING POWER) is reduced to zero for the remainder of an engagement. It is the converse of vulnerability.

FIGHTING STRENGTH
A composite value of FIREPOWER and SURVIVABILITY (defined below) that suitably represents deliverable firepower over the combat life of a UNIT or FORCE. For example, F.W. Lanchester showed that for continuous fire under square-law conditions, what he called FIGHTING STRENGTH of a FORCE could be represented by αA^2 or βB^2; and for linear law conditions by αA or βB. It will be seen that the FIGHTING STRENGTH of a *naval* FORCE using continuous fire with FIGHTING POWER α or

β and STAYING POWER a_1 or b_1 can be represented by a $a_1 \alpha A^2$ or $b_1 \beta B^2$. The object of this study is to seek suitable measures of UNIT and FORCE FIGHTING STRENGTH for salvo fire so that various attributes of warships can be compared.

SCOUTING EFFECTIVENESS. σ_A, σ_B.

The degradation of FIGHTING POWER, measured in hits per salvo, lost due to imperfect detection or tracking of enemy targets. SCOUTING EFFECTIVENESS is a number between 0 and 1 that is the difference between the number of ACCURATE SHOTS delivered with optimal knowledge of enemy composition and location and the number of ACCURATE SHOTS delivered with the existing information.

SUSCEPTIBILITY

The degree to which a target is impotent to take action against ACCURATE SHOTS by the enemy. Total susceptibility results when the target can take no effective actions of maneuver, deception, or hardkill or softkill defense, so that the number of HITS equal the number of ACCURATE SHOTS.

VULNERABILITY

The ease with which a target may be FIREPOWER KILLED (put out of action) by enemy HITS. The converse of VULNERABILITY is STAYING POWER.

KILLABILITY

A composite of SUSCEPTIBILITY and VULNERABILITY.

SURVIVABILITY

The mathematical complement of KILLABILITY. A measure of all defensive actions, including design actions, that reduce SUSCEPTIBILITY and VULNERABILITY (that is, reduce damage and its effects).

COUNTERACTION OR DEFENSIVE POWER

A composite of all defensive actions to reduce SUSCEPTIBILITY to HITS by the enemy. COUNTERACTIONS comprise COUNTERFIRE, SEDUCTION, EVASION, and DISTRACTION.

COUNTERFIRE or HARDKILL COUNTERACTION.
Unit: a_3, b_3. Force: a_3A, b_3B.

Weapon fire by a target to destroy enemy SHOTS. COUNTERFIRE is measured by the number of enemy SHOTS destroyed before they HIT.

SOFT-KILL COUNTERACTIONS

SEDUCTION. Force: a_4, b_4.

The process of causing ACCURATE SHOTS to miss when COUNTER-FIRE has failed, for example, by seduction chaff. SEDUCTION is treated as equally effective against all GOOD SHOTS in a salvo. It is a multiplier applied to COMBAT POWER (defined below) taking values between 0 and 1. The value of a_4 or b_4 may or may not be proportional to the number of surviving targets exercising this mode of soft-kill defense, as appropriate.

EVASION. Force: a_4, b_4.

A process of maneuver to cause GOOD SHOTS to miss. Also design qualities of low-observability that cause GOOD SHOTS to miss. EVASION is treated as equally effective against all GOOD SHOTS in a salvo of, notably, non-homing torpedoes. Mathematically it affects results in the same way as SEDUCTION, and so the same symbol is applied over the same range of values.

DISTRACTION. Force: ρ_A, ρ_B.

A process of causing enemy SHOTS to miss before COUNTERFIRE has its effect. DISTRACTION is treated as equally effective against all SHOTS (GOOD or not) in a salvo. It is a multiplier applied to σ_A or σ_B. The value of ρ may or may not be proportional to the number of surviving targets exercising this mode of soft-kill defense, as appropriate.

COMBAT POWER. $P_A = \alpha A - b_3 B$, $P_B = \beta B - a_3 A$ (in hits per salvo).

The STRIKING POWER of a FORCE minus the total hits eliminated by COUNTERACTIONS of the target FORCE. COMBAT POWER cannot be defined or measured except against a specific enemy FORCE and the COUNTERACTIONS it takes to diminish the STRIKING POWER against it.

Note: The full effect of COMBAT POWER includes the suppression and demoralization of the enemy, but these are treated as of secondary importance in naval combat. For a discussion of the major effects in ground combat, see Hughes [21].

DEFENDER ALERTNESS. δ_A, δ_B.

The extent to which a target UNIT fails to take defensive actions up to its designed combat potential, due to un-readiness or inattention caused by faulty EMCON or condition of readiness. It is normally a multiplier of a_3 or b_3 with values between 0 and 1.

SKILL, or TRAINING, EFFECTIVENESS. τ_A, τ_B.

The degree to which a firing or target UNIT does not reach its designed combat potential, due to inadequate training, organization, or motivation.

COMMAND AND CONTROL

Command and control is a function of command, a process that governs FORCES in a battle, and a system of people and material that perform the function by carrying out the process. It is the command-control (CC) process that is of interest in this study. Because CC governs very nearly all combat actions, its effect must be treated as a modifier of any value in the COMBAT POWER equation. If not readily apparent, it is easily shown that A's CC can diminish his number of participating UNITS, A; his UNIT STRIKING POWER, a_2; his UNIT COUNTERFIRE, a_3; or his SOFT-KILL COUNTERACTIONS, ρ_A or a_4; because STAYING POWER, a_1, is to a large extent inherent in ship design, a CC deficiency probably has least effect on a_1. Because the definitions are structured to represent performance with ideal CC, CC is always a factor deflator, never a force multiplier.

COMBAT WORK. $\Delta B = P_A/b_1$, $\Delta A = P_B/a_1$
(in ships out of action/salvo).

The number of UNITS put out of action by a salvo or a period of continuous fire.

WORK may also be the accumulated UNITS put out of action after a series of salvo exchanges.

COMBAT RESULT. $B[T] = B[0] - \Delta B$, $A[T] = A[0] - \Delta A$.
The conditions existing on both sides at a time T after the battle commenced (time 0). The COMBAT RESULT at time T is the FORCE STRENGTH remaining after subtracting enemy WORK done by that time.

COMBAT OUTCOME

A single-valued measure of the final conditions, or states, of both FORCES when the battle is over. An exchange ratio, $\Delta B/\Delta A$, is a common measure of OUTCOME. In this study the FRACTIONAL EXCHANGE RATIO, defined below, is the preferred MOE for comparing the value of warship attributes.

FRACTIONAL EXCHANGE RATIO. FER = $(\Delta B/B)/(\Delta A/A)$.
COMBAT OUTCOME is measured as the ratio of the fraction of each force remaining at the end of the battle. When the FER is greater than 1, then side A is winning; when the FER is less than 1, then B is winning, in that the winning side will have FORCES with COMBAT POWER remaining when the enemy is impotent. There are pathological exceptions in which both sides' COMBAT POWER is zero, suggesting a draw, but if one side suffers more overkill (computationally negative FORCES remaining) than the other, then the implication is that it has suffered more personnel casualties, greater damage beyond the point of COMBAT KILL, and more ships sunk or sinking.

APPENDIX B. THE AGGREGATION OF TERMS

A thoughtful reader of the assumptions that accompany the salvo model will appreciate their effects on computation, among which are

- The linear degradation of unit capabilities after hits.
- The uniform spread of hits from a salvo over all targets.
- The presumption that force striking power is the product of unit striking power times the number of units and defensive firepower is similarly multiplicative.

The salvo equation expresses a dynamic process in a specific, rigid mathematical construction. One way, perhaps the only way, to escape its strictures and assumptions is to aggregate terms in an even more abstract and primitive formulation. The value of the aggregate terms can be whatever is experimentally true, or best fits the data. For instance, if we observe that the number of hits, $\alpha[2]$, achieved by salvos from two identical warships is only 1.7 of the value of α for one ship, then the striking power of the two is not $\alpha A = \alpha \times 2$ but a nonlinear aggregate value, $\alpha[2] = 1.7 \times \alpha[1]$. If one has experimental evidence for $\alpha[A]$, $A = 1, 2, 3 \ldots$, then he or she can and should use it in the manner now described.

The theoretical structure that follows is adapted from Cares [10]. It is expressed as three "laws of salvo warfare." When the laws describe the process, the general form applies. If and when the particular conditions of linearity also hold (and in general they would not for real combat) then the model forms above would produce true results. If one wishes to deny the assumptions of additivity, then he should retreat into the still more basic form appearing below, using the laws of salvo warfare as guide. He will have to have numerical values for the synthesized terms that the laws imply. Finally, if any of the three laws themselves appear not to hold and must be repudiated, then even this most primitive form is in default.

The First Law of Salvo Warfare: Salvos are interactions of pulses of combat power with their targets and therefore are event-stepped phenomena (not continuous processes) of attrition, in which damage is proportional to the ratio of combat power to staying power. Therefore we say the effect of a salvo by A against B is:

Losses to A = [Combat power of B] / [Staying power of A].

The Second Law of Salvo Warfare: Combat power is the attacker's pulse of lethal energy minus the defender's actions to attenuate the energy. Therefore we say:

[Combat power of B] =
[Striking power of B]-[Defensive power (or Counteractions) of A]

The Third Law of Salvo Warfare: Combat power may be measured in units of hits, staying power in units of hits per ship, and combat potential and damage in units of ships.

Therefore, when the law holds, we need not be concerned with maneuver or advantageous tactical position, or with the effects a salvo might have to demoralize or suppress the enemy's actions. Contrariwise, when the Third Law does not hold, the model is defective. As an example, at the climax of the Battle of Jutland, Admiral Scheer, the German tactical commander, in desperation ordered a torpedo attack by his Third Torpedo-boat Flotilla on the British battle line. The salvo of torpedoes achieved no hits and damage "in units of [battle]ships" was zero. But the combat power visible in the wakes of the torpedoes caused the British commander to turn his battle line away, letting the German battleships escape their awkward posture. The torpedo salvo's effect on Jutland's outcome by briefly suppressing British firepower was very great, even decisive in the view of some historians. When a combat outcome hinges on effects of fighting power other than hits and losses (as it often does in a land battle), then the Third Law is broken and the model is deficient.

A form of the salvo model with aggregated terms may be written that is consistent with the three Laws. Beall [7] and Cares [10] conclude from their research that the following representation of Eq. (3) is the most generally satisfying:

$$\frac{\Delta B}{B} = \frac{\bar{\sigma}_A \bar{\alpha}[A] - \bar{b}_3[B]}{\bar{b}_1[B]}$$

The over-scored symbols represent whole force scouting power, striking power, counteractions, and staying power for the number of units, $[A]$ or $[B]$, attacking or defending. This "four-element model" (Cares' expression [10, p. 25]) is in force-on-force analysis really an eight-element model. Eight elements with the flexibility to aggregate attributes in nonlinear fashion, are superior for *a posteriori* corroboration against the experimental battle results.

However, for exploratory analysis to study individual ship design variants, in the absence of battle data one has little choice but to begin with the assumptions that accompany each of the combat model forms.

APPENDIX C: J. V. CHASE'S EQUATION OF CONTINUOUS FIRE

Developed by Lieutenant (later Rear Admiral) J. V. Chase in 1902 and presented to Cdr. W. McCarty Little for calculating battle outcomes in Naval War College war games, this article was classified Confidential and not declassified until 1972. See Fiske [13, 14].

The equations solved by Chase have been modified here so that the terminology and symbology conform with this work. His original derivation appears *in toto* in Appendix C to Fiske [14].

ASSUMPTIONS

1. Fighting power is delivered in a continuous stream of shell fire.
2. All ships on the same side, A or B, have identical unit fighting power, α or β, and staying power, a_1 or b_1.
3. The value of unit fighting power is constant; that is, it does not change because of a change in target range, target aspect, spotting effectiveness or demoralization.
4. Square-law conditions apply: Every engaged ship is able to fire at every engaged enemy ship and as soon as a ship is out of action the fact is known and fire is shifted to a ship with fighting power remaining.

Force-on-force differential equations for the instantaneous rate at which units are being put out of action at any time t, (*Combat Work* done by the enemy):

$$\frac{dB(t)}{dt} = \frac{\alpha A(t)}{b_1}, \quad \frac{dA(t)}{dt} = \frac{\beta B(t)}{a_1} \qquad (6)$$

State equation for results at any time T:

$$\alpha a_1 \left[A(o)^2 - A(T)^2 \right] = \beta b_1 \left[B(0)^2 - B(T)^2 \right]. \qquad (7)$$

Fighting strengths:
If $\alpha a_1 A^2 > \beta b_1 B^2$, A will win a battle of annihilation.
If $\beta b_1 B^2 > \alpha a_1 A^2$, B will win. $\qquad (8)$

MODEL-BASED CONCLUSIONS

1. From Eq. (8) it is seen that if there are twice as many units on one side as on the other, then for parity each unit of the force with the smaller number of units must be twice as strong in fighting power and twice as strong in staying power as the numerically larger force.

2. From Eq. (7) it is seen that equal increases in fighting power and staying power contribute equally to the fighting strength of a warship.

DISCUSSION

With Eq. (6) we compute combat work done, that is, losses to each side. Lanchester computed combat results, that is, the forces remaining. Consistent with the salvo equations in this article I have retained Chase's formulation of the pair of force-on-force equations. As they have no minus sign in front of the right hand terms, they show not results but work achieved. I have written the state equation solution in Lanchester fashion, which is the result at any time T, rather than work at time T.

The Chase formulation computes losses measured in ships and can be used to explore the value of staying power, as he wished to do. The Lanchester form can only evaluate the aggregate of total forces remaining.

The following retrospective written by Chase in 1921 about his purpose in 1902 seems as apt today as then:

Some years ago when I was a member of the War College Staff, there was considerable discussion among the members of the staff as to the value of concentration of fire. Most of the statements pro and con were couched in vague general terms . . . "glittering generalities." [I] sought some more tangible expression of the advantages to be derived from concentration . . . the term "unit of destruction" is a quantity that does not admit of exact definition but it is readily seen that it serves as a measure of both the offensive and defensive qualities of a ship. By "unit of destruction delivered" by a ship is not meant the units leaving the muzzles of the battery of that ship but "unit delivered" . . . in this way the relative marksmanship of the contending forces may be taken into account.

For example, let there be eight ships originally on each side and let one ship on one side be masked so that $m = 8$ and $n = 7$. Then the eight ships will destroy the seven ships and will have the equivalent of $\sqrt{15}$ (nearly four) intact ships with which to engage the remaining one intact ship . . . it will be seen that after destroying this one intact ship there will remain $\sqrt{14}$. In other words by blanking one ship [temporarily] . . . the eight ships have destroyed an exactly equal force and have remaining the equivalent of 3.74 ships. . . .

... if there be twice as many units on one side as there are on the other, each unit of the force having the smaller number of units must be twice as strong *offensively* and twice as strong *defensively* as one of the hostile units. This has a bearing upon the question of large or small ships.

Inasmuch as the displacement of a ship represents the total weights of the materials composing the ship and borne by her, the various materials could be segregated and transformed into separate masses of such material.

Having certain definite quantities of the various materials the question of ship design [is] . . . in the simplest form: "Shall we construct from these materials *one* ship or *two* ships?" . . . if we decide to build *one* ship instead of *two*, this *single* ship must be twice as strong offensively *and twice* as strong *defensively as one* of the two ships.

It seems to me that while it may be possible to make a ship carry twice as many guns as one of half the displacement it is at least debatable if she can be made twice as strong defensively. The chances of hitting her certainly are much greater and she certainly is not twice as strong defensively against underwater attack.

Chase also noted at the time of his 1902 derivation that the equations applied only to gunfire, and was shrewd enough to observe "that sudden destruction arising from any cause whatsoever will [upset the analysis but] have least effect upon the accuracy of the results . . . if it take place near the end of the engagement. It would seem therefore that the force inferior in gunfire should use the ram or torpedo as early as possible." While he does not develop torpedoes further and reference to ramming bemuses us today, it is probably fair to credit him with an appreciation that a torpedo salvo had to be modeled separately as a pulse of destructiveness with a time delay to account for running time to the targets.

Chase foreshadows the Englishman F. W. Lanchester, and the Russian M. Osipov [31] who rediscover (!) in 1915 the aggregate, greater-than-linear advantage of numerical concentration when square-law conditions obtain. Chase's equations are more powerful than Lanchester's in that not only force size and fighting power variations can be explored but also staying power.

APPENDIX D: CONTRASTS WITH OTHER FORCE-ON-FORCE MODELS
GROUND COMBAT MODELING

The U.S. Army has been more assiduous than the U.S. Navy in attempting to validate its models of combat with historical battle data. There is a broad consensus among analysts that the Lanchester square-law form does not validate well against data, either from exercises or historical battles. This need not deter the use of continuous fire or salvo fire models for the study of naval combat. The square-law conditions rarely hold for ground combat, but usually do for naval combat. In ground combat the defender secures a unit firepower advantage by exploiting terrain and employing prepared positions. Unless the defender advantage is taken into account in model validation, a square-law model of ground combat will not conform with historical battle data. The problem vanishes at sea because there is no corresponding advantage of terrain or fortification. Second, the Lanchester model, which measures casualties produced by fire, inherently presumes that the only significant achievement of fire is casualties, and so victory must be expressed in casualties. But one of the most important effects of firepower in ground combat is suppression of enemy fire and movement, and a commonly observed cause of mission success is the domination or control of the enemy without severe attrition. There is no counterpart in naval combat. At sea, battles are won by putting enemy warships out of action and victory is measured by warships sunk. The first mathematical models of combat were developed by naval officers for the analysis of attrition by gunfire because the conditions in the model fit the conditions of a naval battle. This is still the case today.

OTHER APPROACHES USING SIMPLE MATHEMATICS OF COMBAT

Two best-known analytic approaches to exploratory, or descriptive, force-on-force analysis are Lanchester equations and stochastic duels, both of which are well developed and have extensive literature. See, for example, J. G. Taylor [34] for the former and Thomas [36], or Ancker [38] for the latter. Neither approach is suitable for modern naval combat because neither captures the essential elements of modern naval salvo warfare.

A third, less well-known approach is by T. C. Taylor. His unpublished article [35] is interesting, very much to the subject and insightful in many respects. T. C. Taylor treats offensive and defensive combat power as a fraction of enemy capability. He defines:

E_{OB} as the fraction of side A's tactical potential destroyed by B's salvo in the absence of defensive measures by A.

E_{DA} is the fraction of E_{OB} eliminated by A's defense, so that the fraction of A's combat power remaining after B's salvo is

$$F_{AR} = 1 - [E_{OB} (1 - E_{DA})].$$

F_{AR} is defined symmetrically for A's salvo effectiveness against B.

The Taylor formulation can be manipulated with some interesting analytical results, but the use of fractions sometimes conceals important effects and is not trustworthy for the objectives of this study.

REFERENCES

[1] Ancker, C. J., Jr., *One-on-One Stochastic Duels.* ORSA MAS, Washington, DC, 1982.

[2] Ball, R. E., *The Fundamentals of Aircraft Combat Survivability Analysis and Design.* AIAA Inc., New York, 1985.

[3] Ball, R. E. and Calvano, C. N., *The Fundamentals of Surface Ship Combat Survivability Analysis and Design*, draft, US Naval Postgraduate School, Monterey, CA, 1994.

[4] Bankes, S. C., "Exploratory Modeling and the Use of Simulation for Policy Analysis," RAND Note No. N-3093-A, Rand Corporation, Santa Monica, CA, 1992.

[5] Barr, D., Weir, M., and Hoffman, J., "Evaluation of Combat," US Naval Postgraduate School, Monterey, CA, 1991.

[6] Baudry, A., *The Naval Battle: Studies of Tactical Factors*, Hughes Rees, Ltd., London, 1914.

[7] Beall, T. R., "The Development of a Naval Battle Model and Its Validation Using Historical Data," Masters Thesis, US Naval Postgraduate School, Monterey, CA, 1990.

[8] Bernotti, R., *Fundamentals of Naval Tactics*, Naval Institute Press, Annapolis, MD, 1912.

[9] Brzozowsky, K. W., and Memmesheimer, R. M., "The Application of the Sochard Ship Damage Model to World War II Ship Damage," unpublished NSWC monograph, White Oak, MD, 1988.

[10] Cares, J. R., "The Fundamentals of Salvo Warfare," Masters Thesis, US Naval Postgraduate School, Monterey, CA, 1990.

[11] Chase, J. V., "A Mathematical Investigation of the Effect of Superiority of Force in Combats Upon the Sea," unpublished CONFIDENTIAL paper, 1902, declassified and printed in Appendix C to Fiske [13].

[12] Epstein, J. M., "The Calculus of Conventional War: Dynamic Analysis Without Lanchester Theory," The Brookings Institution, Washington, DC, 1985.

[13] Fiske, B. A., "American Naval Policy," *U.S. Naval Institute Proceedings*, March, 1905.

[14] Fiske, B. A., *The Navy as a Fighting Machine*, originally published 1916, reissued in Classics of Sea Power Series, Naval Institute Press. Annapolis, MD, 1988.

[15] Gafarian, A. V., and Ancker, C. J., Jr., "The Two-on-One Stochastic Duel," *Naval Research Logistics* (1984).

[16] Galvin, B. R. "Punching Combat's Equations," *U.S. Naval Institute Proceedings*, July 1991.

[17] Hansen, I. and Gray, H. P., "Passive Protection and Ship Survivability in Years 2005–2020," David Taylor Research Center Report SSPD 90-174-41, Bethesda, MD, May 1990. CONFIDENTIAL

[18] Hatzopoulis. E., "A Modern Naval Combat Model," Masters Thesis, US Naval Postgraduate School, Monterey, CA, 1990.

[19] Horrigan. T. J., "The Configural Theory of Weapons Effectiveness: A Means to Enhance the Impact of Technology on Combat Effectiveness," Horrigan Analytics, 1460 N. Sandburg Terrace, Chicago, IL, January, 1988.

[20] Hughes, W. P., Jr., *Fleet Tactics: Theory and Practice*, Naval Institute Press, Annapolis, MD, 1986.

[21] Hughes, W. P., Jr., "Combat Science: An Organizing Study," Research Paper, US Naval Postgraduate School, Monterey, CA. 1992.

[22] Hughes, W. P., Jr., "The Value of Warship Attributes in Missile Combat." U.S. Naval Postgraduate School Report NPS-OR-93-00 I, October 1992.

[23] Hughes, W. P., Jr., "The Military Worth of Staying Power," Draft Research Study, US Naval Postgraduate School, Monterey, CA, 1993.

[24] Humphrey, R. L, "Warship Damage Rules for Naval Wargaming," ORSA/TIMS Joint Meeting, Las Vegas, NV, May 1990.

[25] Humphrey, R. L, "Damage and Losses of Warships in Modern Combat," ORSA/TIMS Joint Meeting, Anaheim, CA, November 1991.

[26] Lalis, A. P., "Sensitivity Analysis of the Modern Naval Combat Model," Masters Thesis, US Naval Postgraduate School, Monterey, CA, 1991.

[27] Mahan, A. T., *The Lessons of the War with Spain*, Little Brown, Boston, MA, 1898.

[28] Mahan, A. T., *Naval Strategy, Compared and Contrasted with the Principles and Practices of Military Operations on Land*, Little Brown, Boston, MA, 1911.

[29] McKearney, T. J., "The Solomons Naval Campaign: A Paradigm for Surface Warships in Maritime Strategy," Masters Thesis, US Naval Postgraduate School, Monterey, CA, 1985.

[30] Morse, P. M. and Kimball, G. E., *Methods of Operations Research*, The M.I.T. Press, Cambridge, MA, First Edition. Revised, 1951.

[31] Osipov, M., "The Influence of the Numerical Strength of Engaged Forces on Their Casualties." Originally in Russian, Military Collection, 1915: Translated by R. A. Helmold and A. S. Rehm and republished as U.S. Army CAA Research Paper CAA-RP-91-2, Bethesda, MD, 1991.

[32] Smith, T. T., "Combat Modeling Low Intensity Conflict Anti-Surface Warfare for Engagement Analysis," SECRET Masters Thesis. US Naval Postgraduate School, Monterey, CA. 1991.

[33] Snell, R. L. "Countertargeting in Modern Naval Combat," Masters Thesis, US Naval Postgraduate School, Monterey, CA, 1991.

[34] Taylor, J. G., *Lanchester Models of Warfare*, ORSA MAS, Washington, DC, 2 volumes, 1983.

[35] Taylor, T. C., "A Salvo Exchange Model for Modern Tactical Conditions," unpublished article. 16546 Chalet Terrace, Pacific Palisades, CA 90272, Revision 5, July 1990.

[36] Thomas, C. J., *Military Operations Research Course: Selected Topics of Military Operations.* WORC-ORSA, 1966.

[37] Thomas, C. J., "Verification Revisited." in *Military Modeling* (2nd ed.), MORS, Alexandria, VA, 1989.

[38] US Army DARCOM. *Engineering Design Handbook*, DARCOM-P 706-101, Part One, Alexandria, VA 1977.

APPENDIX B
THE SALVO EQUATIONS
AND FORCE PLANNING

Annex E of the U.S. Navy Warfare Publication (NWP) 5-01, *Navy Planning*, contains the approved process for assessing risk in naval combat, the Relative Combat Power Analysis (RCPA) process. Since the word "salvo" appears nowhere in the entire NWP, it should not surprise the reader that the salvo equations are absent from the assessment process as well. In fact, the document's recommendation is to abandon mathematical calculations and rely on a "rich dialogue" between staff members for a subjective risk assessment. Their guidance is based on the mistaken belief that the only mathematical approach possible must be borrowed from land combat analysis, whose force ratio calculations they deem "insufficient for maritime use."[1] Chapter 1 and appendix A amply prove that naval warfare does in fact have its own mathematical models. This appendix details a process for using them in fleet level planning for war at sea.[2]

RCPA PROCEDURE FOR SALVO WARFARE

1. *Order of Battle (OOB) Analysis.* The fleet intelligence officer (N2) should determine the likely Red OOB, against which the fleet operations officer (N3) should propose a Blue OOB. Since OOBs are simply lists of platforms to commit to a fight, these lists must be converted to the appropriate forms of naval power: offensive combat power, defensive combat power, and staying power.

Offensive Combat Power: For each platform, assess how many antiship missiles will be fired in the first salvo. Total these for the entire force and call this value O. Include any specific salvo doctrine that applies. List the thousand-pound bomb equivalent (TPBE) rating for each missile. Compute for both Red and Blue. N2 and N3 should provide these estimates.

Defensive Combat Power: For each platform, assess how many anti-ship missiles can be defeated by all defensive systems (hardkill and soft-kill). Call this value D. Be consistent in how area defense and point defense are counted. For example, area defense missiles are more subject to poor distribution of fire than point defense systems. Also, point defense systems work only in a short time window, so multiple engagements might not be possible. In addition, be careful of how decoys are counted: to a shooter, a decoy that appears to be a ship will get a ship's share of the salvo. Otherwise, it will defeat only one missile. Compute for both Red and Blue. N2 and N3 should provide these estimates.

Staying Power: Using the cube root rule, assess how many TPBEs each hull on either side can withstand. List and save the TPBE details for future calculations, and also determine SP, the total staying power of each force. Staying power is simply the total number of hits required to sink a force. Compute for both Red and Blue. N2 and N4 should provide the tonnage data.

2. *Analyze the Combat Power Exchange.* The result of the exchange of combat power is measured by the number of leakers, L. Strictly speaking, if $O > D$, then $O - D > 0$ and the exchange will result in $L = O - D$. If $O < D$, then $O - D < 0$ and $L = 0$ (there will be no leakers). With very large salvos and forces close to parity, however, prudent planners will need to account for randomness in the salvo exchange before assessing damage.

3. *Analyze Leakage Rate.* As discussed in chapter 1, combat entropy measures how random disorder in a salvo exchange makes outcomes deviate from statistical expectations. Although naval operations research has identified the sources of combat entropy and determined a way to characterize it, research has not determined how a given level of combat entropy correlates with the specific ways that the salvo exchange will be disordered. However, we should at least assume that not all offensive shots will hit their intended targets, and that there will likely be more leakers than step 2 indicates. In the absence of better research, a reasonable approach to help

staff planners explore how combat entropy might impact the fight is to apply a *leakage rate (l)*, with a value between 0 and 1. The revised number of leakers would then be

$$(O + (O \times l)) - D.$$

Since *l* is the most arbitrary part of this assessment, it would be wise to explore the salvo exchange at different *l* levels, perhaps at equal intervals centered on *l* or from 0 up to *l*. Later in this appendix we provide an example of a range of *l* from 0.0 to 0.3.

4. *Assess Damage.* Damage at the force level, *K*, is nothing more than

$$K = \frac{L}{SP}.$$

This is assessed from both Blue and Red perspectives and is a very quick and helpful way to conduct a comparative analysis of different force packages and against different enemy OOBs. Since many missions depend on certain platforms surviving a salvo attack, staff planners should also want to know how specific ships might be affected during an exchange. While this is not as straightforward as analyzing force damage, it can be accomplished almost as quickly using the random number generator in Microsoft Excel and some very basic spreadsheet skills. First, create a set of intervals, each equal to 1/H, where H is the number of hulls on a side. Select a random number between 0 and 1 and assign a hit to the ship associated with the interval into which the random number falls.[3] Repeat this *L* times, and then calculate damage to individual ships based on staying power depletion for each hit. The spreadsheet can be run multiple times to see how the damage spreads out among the hulls. Since many force packages have multiple ships of the same class, the damage will often be similar, with the only difference being the hull numbers hit, not a change in the amount of combat power lost. Do not avoid assigning more hits to a ship than are indicated in the TPBE list—this is a key component of combat entropy as well.

SAMPLE RELATIVE COMBAT POWER ASSESSMENT

1. *OOB Analysis.* Suppose A and B consist of the following:

Side A	A	a_3	a_1^*
DDG1	6	4	2
DDG2	6	4	2

Side A	A	a_3	a_1*
DDG3	6	4	2
DDG4	6	4	2
FFG1	4	2	1
FFG2	4	2	1

* In TPBEs
$O_A = 32$
$D_A = 20$
$SP_A = 10$

Side B	B	b_3	b_1*
DDG1	6	4	2
DDG2	6	4	2
DDG3	6	4	2
DDG4	6	4	2
FFG1	4	2	2
FFG2	4	2	2

* In TPBEs
$O_B = 24$
$D_B = 28$
$SP_B = 12$

2. Analyze the Combat Power Exchange.

Side A: $L_A = 24 - 20 = 4$

Side B: $L_B = 32 - 28 = 4$

3. Analyze Leakage Rate.

Side A: *Leaker Rate (%)**

	0	10	20	30
L_A	4	6	9	11

* Rounded to the nearest whole number.

Side B: *Leaker Rate (%)**

	0	10	20	30
L_B	4	7	10	14

* Rounded to the nearest whole number.

4. *Assess Damage.*

Force Damage:

Leaker Rate (%)

	0	10	20	30
K_A	40%	60%	90%	100%
K_B	33%	58%	83%	100%

Individual Ship Damage: Hit Distribution (Five Trials, 0% Leaker Rate)					
Side A	*Trial 1*	*Trial 2*	*Trial 3*	*Trial 4*	*Trial 5*
DDG1	0	2	2	0	2
DDG2	0	0	0	1	1
DDG3	2	0	0	0	0
DDG4	1	0	1	2	0
FFG1	1	1	0	1	1
FFG2	0	1	1	0	0
Side B	*Trial 1*	*Trial 2*	*Trial 3*	*Trial 4*	*Trial 5*
DDG1	0	0	0	0	0
DDG2	2	2	0	1	0
DDG3	0	1	0	1	1
DDG4	1	1	3	1	2
FFG1	0	0	0	1	1
FFG2	1	0	1	0	0

Individual Ship Damage: Hit Distribution (Five Trials, 20% Leaker Rate)					
Side A	*Trial 1*	*Trial 2*	*Trial 3*	*Trial 4*	*Trial 5*
DDG1	1	0	2	1	1
DDG2	2	2	2	3	3
DDG3	3	2	3	0	0
DDG4	2	4	0	1	0
FFG1	1	1	1	4	4
FFG2	0	0	1	0	1

Side B	Trial 1	Trial 2	Trial 3	Trial 4	Trial 5
DDG1	1	1	3	2	5
DDG2	1	2	1	0	0
DDG3	2	2	2	3	1
DDG4	3	3	0	3	1
FFG1	1	1	3	0	2
FFG2	2	1	1	2	1

5. *Relative Combat Power Assessment.* On inspection, it is clear that although both sides have the same number of ships, side A has the stronger offense, but side B has the stronger defense and staying power. In addition, side B's offense and defense are both assessed to be more reliable than side A's. Despite these differences, both sides of the salvo exchange should produce the same number of leakers. However, the number of leakers for each side at leakage rates of 0 percent, 10 percent, 20 percent, and 30 percent are investigated.[4]

At the force level, damage calculations give a slight advantage to side B in the exchange up until the 30 percent leaker rate, at which point both defenses are completely saturated.[5] The individual hit tables show how those leakers might be distributed at the 0 percent and 20 percent levels.[6] A statistical analysis would look at a very large number of trials to get an overall average number of hits assigned to each ship. That is not the intention here: simple division will show that the average number of hits per hull would be 2/3, which would never happen in any single case. Each battle can have only one outcome, however, so it is more important for planners to have some idea of patterns in the hit distribution than to know the average number of hits per hull.

Five trials are shown, but planners should conduct as many trials as it takes for them to feel confident that they understand the dominant patterns. For example, with only five trials, it seems likely that side A should expect one of its DDGs and one of its FFGs to be put out of action, and another of its DDGs to withstand 50 percent damage (although which particular hulls are impacted might change). Similarly, side B should expect one DDG out of action, and one DDG and one FFG damaged. If planning time allows, more trials can be examined, but these patterns are already discernable.

By contrast, at the 20 percent leaker rate the first three trials for side A suggest that three of four DDGs will be put out of action as well as one of two FFGs. The last two trials show significant overkill of one of the FFGs, such that too many hits are distributed away from the DDGs, putting only one of four DDGs out of action and damaging one. In this case planners will most certainly want to examine more trials to see which of these two patterns will be dominant. A similar statement can be made about the hit distribution for side B at a 20 percent leaker rate.

APPENDIX C
DECONSTRUCTING C4ISR

The goal of this appendix is not to reclassify military command-and-control functions under new terms but to show how fleet operations are poorly served by prevailing concepts of automated, centralized decision making. It will simplify C4ISR for operational-level naval warfare by reducing it to just two detection functions, search and surveillance.

THE MODERN MODEL OF C4ISR

Since its inception in the late 1990s under the rubric of network-centric warfare, the dogma has persisted that a highly centralized combat system with modern networking, computing, and artificial intelligence will completely trivialize detection and engagement of enemy targets. Figure C.1 is a graphic representation of this model, which should be instantly recognizable to anyone with recent experience in the Pentagon or in C4ISR-related industries. It also should be familiar to others as a digitization and simplification of the OODA (observe, orient, decide, act) decision-making loop.

According to adherents of centralized C4ISR, dominance in modern warfare comes from deploying a grid of hundreds of manned and unmanned sensors over a wide area containing a set of perhaps thousands of enemy targets. This sensor grid will supposedly detect all militarily relevant targets in the target grid and then pass each target to a centralized computer system in which sophisticated algorithms will optimize the assignment of weapons from a weapons grid to each target. The entire set of processes is to be enabled by a theater-wide information backplane—that is, a secure communications and computer network.[1]

This concept has many technological and information theoretic problems, but its most unrealistic aspect is that which is most dear to the operator: tactics are excluded from the system altogether. The precepts of centralized C4ISR assume away the physical realities of time and space, valuing information and data flow over the positioning of combat assets and people.[2] Centralized C4ISR adherents have claimed that they can do without physical tactics because they expect exceptionally enhanced performance from "networked effects" (a term poorly defined in doctrine).

In almost two decades of fleet experience, the claims behind the stylized descriptions of these processes have not been proven, and neither have any of the technical superlatives that they require been confirmed. Blind faith in the power of automated, centralized C4ISR has nonetheless escaped an appropriate level of scrutiny, particularly for naval operational level of war decision making. Because so much confusion derives from combining a host of challenging technical, theoretical, and organizational issues into what is often a fashionable catchphrase, it is time that the C4ISR terms were disintegrated to stand alone and be reevaluated for use by fleet staffs and flag officers.

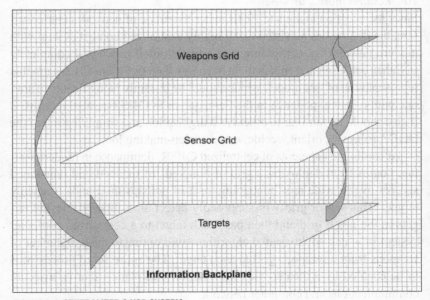

FIGURE C.1 CENTRALIZED C4ISR SYSTEM

DECONSTRUCTING TERMS

COMMAND

At sea, command is simple, straightforward, traditional, and legal: it is both the authority over and the responsibility for people and things. Those who advocate automated, centralized command confuse the communications function of *issuing* commands with *commanding*. There is nothing inherently electronic or automated about command at sea—a flag officer is still very much in command even when electronics fail. *Recommendation*: Remove "command" from the acronym C4ISR.

CONTROL

Figure C.1 describes a system in which coarse-scale actors can control fine-scale actions. It is worth noting that the early developers of this model of warfare came from the U.S. Air Force and U.S. Navy aviation communities. In this environment, the medium is thin, targets have hard reflective surfaces, and the primary means of detection—advanced radar systems—can transmit at very high frequency and very high power to get very exact positions for all targets in the field of view. In fact, network-centric warfare concepts were conceived soon after advanced digital detection and tracking systems (like the U.S. Aegis air defense system) were fielded, and early renditions of network-centric warfare looked like extrapolations of these systems to other domains. Compared to most of the tasks required for operational level of war commanders at sea, the air warfare subset is much simpler and readily lends itself to fine-scale control by coarse-scale decision makers. But the naval environment and naval target set are far more complex than those in air warfare, particularly at the operational level of war. The following contrasting examples show how.

Consider the tasks of one of the most junior air defense operators in the fleet, an air-search radar scope monitor. A watchstander's tasks are fairly simple: observe digitized radar returns, ensure they are properly identified and represented by the correct digital icons, and report anything important about targets to a supervisor. The tracking supervisor, a relatively senior enlisted watchstander, receives these reports and monitors the icons for a number of junior scope operators. The ship's tactical action officer coordinates with the tracking supervisor as well as with supervisors tracking targets with surface and subsurface detection systems. This officer also reports to a force-wide air defense officer who monitors the reports and targets of all the ships in a force, each of which has nearly identical air defense tracking teams. The force air defense officer reports to the flag watchstanders, who monitor air defense for the admiral. Each of these watchstanders—indeed, even the admiral—sees an identical view of the environment. Scientists call such systems "scale invariant" with simple information conditions because they appear identical at all scales of observation. Information can be collected and control measures applied centrally in scale invariant systems.

Consider the tasks of one of the most junior antisubmarine warfare watchstanders. This person might be interpreting a very complicated sonar display, designed to unveil very specific information about one particular aspect of a target submarine's detectability. There are usually a few such operators who are monitored by a sonar tracking supervisor. This supervisor interprets what each display operator sees and ensures the correct icon is entered into the ship's combat system, in coordination with the tactical action officer. This officer ensures the information is conveyed to a more senior staff, usually a destroyer squadron, who combines the ship's report with information that it might have received from other ships, submarines, and aircraft conducting antisubmarine operations in the area. The squadron watchstanders report to the flag staff, who monitor antisubmarine warfare for the admiral. These operators and supervisors are working with complex information conditions because almost none of them have the same display (especially at the most junior level). Displays for the most junior watchstanders are the most detailed, while those at successively more senior watches are coarser and coarser compilations of less and less detail.[3] Scientists would call this a multiscale system with complex information conditions.

The primary feature of multiscale systems is that they are best observed and controlled at the scale at which important patterns emerge, not from a central authority. It is not that these systems are uncontrollable by the fleet staff, just that the kind of fine-scale control described in figure C.1 is an illusion when information conditions are complex (that is, for most of naval warfare). These cases require decentralized control in which coarse-scale statements of the commander's intent inform finer-scale decisions.

This notion of control has a long tradition in the navy and has had a recent rebirth as the U.S. Army concept of "mission command."[4] *Recommendation*: Remove "control" from the acronym C4ISR.

COMMUNICATIONS

Advanced digital communications seemed exotic twenty years ago, and many thought wars of the future would be won or lost on the talents of a specially trained officer class of IT network professionals. It seemed logical to some to elevate it to the same rank as command and control (indeed, the acronym used to be just "C2" until networking gained its equality). But like many other naval innovations, technical maturity and widespread use turned a complicated apparatus that was once too sophisticated for most warfighters to understand into an appliance operated and maintained by well-trained junior enlisted. At the fleet level, IT now has about the same status as internal combustion engines—impossible to get along without but so commonplace as to be just another part of the fighting machine.

There is but one way that communications ought to be planned and managed at the highest levels, and that is in signal discipline. Most fleet communicators would claim they have a bandwidth problem, but what they really have is a linguistics problem. Too much bandwidth in peacetime has allowed communications to get sloppy and long-winded. When bandwidth was truly limited before the advent of IT, navies had many techniques to communicate effectively, such as prowords, flag action tables, and other brevity schemes. All fleet traffic is reverting to plain language, with the effect that ever more chatter immediately consumes whatever new bandwidth a fleet receives. Enforcing signals discipline, however, is more in the realm of how a senior trains sailors to talk about how they fight, and not an IT function. *Recommendation*: Remove "communications" from the acronym C4ISR.

COMPUTERS

Proponents of artificial intelligence (AI) and "big data" analytics would have us believe that militaries worldwide are on the verge of providing a new age of automated decision making. While computers have been a part of tactical naval warfare since before World War II (the Ford Mark 1 electro-mechanical analog gunfire computer is a prime example), it was only when advanced, high-speed digital communications offered a way to link *all* tactical-level digital computers within a force that concepts of centralized command-and-control "computing" came to prominence. While one might easily understand how the digital grandson of the Mark 1 computes gunfire ballistics or how a digitally steered phased-array radar tracks a target, it is far more difficult to understand how hundreds, if not thousands, of similar inputs are combined in the modern C4ISR model.

The gunfire and radar computers are well-understood by their operators because these computers and operators are working on well-bounded local problems with local information. If these two computers share information with each other, however, then there must be some kind of digital interpreter to make sure the information is used correctly by both systems. Neither the gunfire nor the radar operators need to know how each other's computer works, but someone in a supervisory role (perhaps the tactical action officer) must understand both computers and the translation. Connecting more computers requires more complicated interpreters in more places. Engineering these interpreters is not too difficult as long as the tasks common to all the computers are consistent with each other and locally bounded.[5] But all this exquisite engineering still requires supervisors who understand each individual component as well as the translated whole. This is possible, as discussed earlier, because systems with local information and a well-bounded problem are scale invariant with simple information conditions. Proficiency at these roles is acquired only after months of technical school and years of experience.

As combat rises above the tactical level, there might be thousands of networked computers with thousands of operators all laboring on some part of the operational problem. These are now multiscale systems with complex information conditions. Simple data translators are no longer sufficient, so proponents of automated C4ISR advocate centralized computers with sophisticated heuristics to create operational-level meaning from tactical data. But computers can only compute—they are incapable of the kind of independent, imaginative thinking that humans have. Computers can only invoke some of a very large set of mathematical or statistical techniques developed by humans.

Which ones work best is a function of the information, not the heuristic itself, and there is not one best "universal algorithm" for solving all problems. So exactly what is "decided" by a high-level decision support system is obscure to fleet planners and flag officers and is usually understood only by the scientists who created it, often years in advance of an operation in which it was employed. There may or may not be a useful algorithm within their "black box," but unlike at the tactical level, they have neither the schooling nor the experience to do anything more than blindly accept what centralized computers tell them. Moreover, anyone who has played video games against a computer adversary knows it is possible by repeated observation to reverse engineer how the computer thinks. If AI and big data enthusiasts think they can create heuristics that are complex enough to solve complex operational level of war problems completely, then they must also believe that heuristics can be developed to defeat these techniques, so competition between centralized, computerized decision making should result in electronic stalemate in the long run. It is best to relegate these systems to a support role, and only when fleet staff officers perfectly understand how they think. In combat at the operational level of war, imagination and complex thinking should be left to admirals and their staffs. *Recommendation*: Remove "computers" from the acronym C4ISR.

INTELLIGENCE

C4ISR doctrine has "intelligence" lumped in with surveillance and reconnaissance, as if they were all coequally planned, managed, and automated detection functions. This view comes from too many years of peacetime intelligence gathering, when the goal was to develop an encyclopedic knowledge of an adversary, often very technical in nature. But wartime intelligence work is more properly the intellectual process of interpreting, inferring, or deducing what an enemy is or might be doing than it is the product of an automated information-gathering process. Fleet-level intelligence activities that support a fleet in combat are much too important to be relegated to a perfunctory role in a monolithic electronic system—in fact, intelligence doctrine itself rejects that notion. Moreover, intelligence identifies and prioritizes what surveillance and reconnaissance efforts should look for, and intelligence data comes from surveillance or reconnaissance; they cannot be coequals. *Recommendation:* Remove "intelligence" from the acronym C4ISR.

SURVEILLANCE AND RECONNAISSANCE

Doctrine uses "surveillance" and "reconnaissance" interchangeably, and many doctrinal publications fail to even define these terms. To confound matters further, doctrine often describes surveillance as part of reconnaissance. Search, a detection process that is well established (both operationally and theoretically), is all but forgotten by doctrine. Chapter 2 makes the case in detail that there are only two primary detection functions, surveillance and search, which must be planned and managed quite differently from each other. *Recommendation*: "Surveillance and reconnaissance" should be replaced by "surveillance and search," and those terms are important enough to stand unabbreviated. No acronym is needed.

APPENDIX D
DISTRIBUTED COMBAT POWER:
APPLICATION OF SALVO THEORY
TO UNMANNED SYSTEMS
BY JEFFREY R. CARES[1]

1.1 INTRODUCTION

The U.S. Navy's littoral combat ship (LCS) was originally conceived as a small platform that would leverage networking and unmanned systems to fundamentally change how ships fight in some of the most demanding maritime scenarios, particularly in cluttered lethal environments just off shore. In early analyses, it was thought that severing the physical connection between this warship's combat power and its hull would be the main source of advantage for the LCS in naval combat. As a fielded program, however, the LCS has focused on different capabilities and leverage points, and while unmanned systems and modularity are still integral to platform, they have not been as important an element to the LCS's operational prowess as originally intended. Part of the reason for this is that unmanned systems technology has not progressed enough for the LCS to meet its full promise in this regard. As the technology improves, however, the opportunity still exists for the LCS to become a revolutionary innovation in naval warfare. This chapter introduces a variant of Hughes' salvo equations to show how distributing and reconfiguring combat power among a group of LCS platforms can dramatically improve the LCS's ability to fight, survive, and fight again in high-end antiship missile combat. These results extend beyond naval warfare to any operational concept for unmanned systems in which host platforms control large numbers of independent, distributable, unmanned vehicles.

1.2 SALVO THEORY

The classic form of naval warfare is the gunnery duel, a contest in which combatants apply continuous fire (increments of combat power applied over time) from large-caliber guns against their foes. The primary physical process in a gunnery duel is an incremental depletion of the resistant force of the targeted hull, or staying power. Mathematical models of the gunnery duel were first developed more than one hundred years ago and are well known to operations research analysts.

There are other types of naval weapons—rams, mines, torpedoes, bombs, and missiles—in which destructive power arrives instantaneously and in much larger increments. The form changes from continuous fire to pulse fire. Until World War II, pulse-fire weapons were considered secondary batteries; continuous fire from large-caliber guns held center stage. World War II saw the end of big guns as a navy's main offensive capability. Air-delivered pulses of power—from both airplanes and missiles—became the central focus of fleets, but an accompanying mathematical model took decades to germinate. Although developed almost thirty years ago, this "new" model, Hughes' salvo equations, remains obscure to most naval operations research analysts, mostly because they favor probabilistic simulations of specific warfare scenarios over theoretical mathematical excursions. This appendix shows, however, that a theoretical exploration of naval combat using a variant of the salvo equations is very useful in identifying sources of advantage in a new age of naval warfare that employs large numbers of unmanned systems.

1.3 THE SALVO EQUATIONS

The salvo equations, force-on-force equations for pulse combat, describe the damage inflicted by one side against another in a pulse-weapon salvo (as a fraction of total pre-salvo force) as

$$\frac{\Delta A}{A} = \frac{\beta B - a_3 A}{a_1 A} \quad , \quad \frac{\Delta B}{B} = \frac{\alpha A - b_3 B}{b_1 B} \qquad \text{[Eq. 1.1]}$$

where

A = Number of units in force A

B = Number of units in force B

α = Number of missiles fired by each A unit (offensive combat power)

β = Number of missiles fired by each B unit (offensive combat power)

a_1 = Number of hits by B's missiles needed to put one A out of action (staying power)

b_1 = Number of hits by A's missiles needed to put one B out of action (staying power)

a_3 = Number of attacking missiles that can be destroyed by each A (defensive combat power)

b_3 = Number of attacking missiles that can be destroyed by each B (defensive combat power)

ΔA = Number of units in force A out of action from B's salvo

ΔB = Number of units in force B out of action from A's salvo

Note that a two-way salvo exchange is expected (there is one equation for side A and one for side B).

Consider two competing three-ship task groups, side A and side B. Assume these ships are identical in every way and have the following characteristics: $\alpha = \beta = 4$, $a_1 = b_1 = 2$, $a_3 = b_3 = 3$. Then after a single salvo,

$$\frac{\Delta B}{B} = \frac{\Delta A}{A} = \frac{4(3) - 3(3)}{2(3)} = \frac{12 - 9}{6} = 0.50, \text{ or } 50\%. \qquad \text{[Eq. 1.2]}$$

Fifty percent damage means each side will lose half its force, or the equivalent of 1.5 ships.

Alternatively, if there is only one ship on side B while side A still has three, then

$$\frac{\Delta B}{B} = \frac{4(3) - 3(1)}{2(1)} = \frac{12 - 3}{2} = 4.50, \qquad \text{[Eq. 1.3]}$$

$$\frac{\Delta A}{A} = \frac{4(1) - 3(3)}{2(3)} = \frac{4 - 9}{6} = -0.83.$$

This means that B loses its single ship (actually, this one ship could be destroyed 4.5 times over) and A loses none (a negative amount of damage means less than 0 percent are damaged).

The equations can be iterated to explore sequences of salvos during an ongoing battle. For example, assume $A = B = 3$, $\alpha = 3$, $\beta = 4$, $a_1 = 3$, $b_1 = 2$, $a_3 = 3$ and $b_3 = 2$. Then after a single salvo,

$$\frac{\Delta B}{B} = \frac{3(3) - 3(2)}{2(3)} = \frac{9 - 6}{6} = 0.50, \qquad \text{[Eq. 1.4]}$$

$$\frac{\Delta A}{A} = \frac{4(3) - 3(3)}{3(3)} = \frac{12 - 9}{9} = 0.33.$$

B loses 1.5 ships and A loses only one. If the surviving ships attack each other with a second salvo, then

$$\frac{\Delta B}{B} = \frac{3(2) - 2(1.5)}{2(1.5)} = \frac{6 - 3}{3} = 1.00, \qquad \text{[Eq. 1.5]}$$

$$\frac{\Delta A}{A} = \frac{4(1.5) - 3(1.5)}{3(2)} = \frac{6 - 4.5}{6} = 0.25.$$

B loses its remaining force while A loses only half a ship (a quarter of a two-ship force).

1.4 INTERPRETING DAMAGE

What are we to make of results like "destroyed 4.5 times over," "negative damage," or "losing half a ship"? Predicting damage at sea has always been difficult. In the era of big guns, analysts could calculate how many shells must impact an enemy's ship to exhaust its staying power, but there were frequently unexpected cases of, say, a single lucky round hitting a magazine, inability to control fires or flooding or disabled interior communications that contributed to a shorter combat life than the equations might prescribe. Given that catastrophic failures occurred with the relatively smaller increments of combat power from guns, it is no surprise that these effects are even more pronounced in salvo warfare. The exact outcomes from salvo exchanges are indeed exceptionally unpredictable.

Salvo equations are best used, then, for comparative analysis rather than predictive analysis. Very useful aspects of war at sea can be explored with this perspective, such as force sufficiency, salvo size selection, the relative strength of offense against a certain defense, fractional exchange ratios, and so on. For example, inflicting 4.5 times more damage than required is one way to overcome the extreme variability in actual results: such a high level of overkill leaves much less to chance than a perfectly sized salvo. For reasons that will be discussed later, however, this also suggests that some missiles must be wasted in this effort to reduce uncertainty. Comparative analysis allows this tradeoff (overkill versus wasted shots) to be quantitatively addressed.

The usual way that damage is assessed by the salvo equations is pro rata. For example, while in actual combat, a three-ship force might incur

50 percent damage a variety of ways (one and a half ships damaged, three ships each with 50 percent damage, two ships with 75 percent damage and one with none, etc.), for comparative analysis, the analyst does not need to make that distinction. Explicitly, equation 1.1 is saying that when two forces exchange salvos, then damage per ship ($\Delta B/B$ or $\Delta A/A$) stems from the interaction of three factors: offensive combat power (αA or βB), defensive combat power ($b_3 B$ or $a_3 A$) and staying power ($b_1 B$ or $a_1 A$). We decrement units of offensive combat power by units of defensive combat power and apply the remaining offensive combat power (if there is any) directly to staying power. Since combat power is resident in the hull, perhaps in tubes, launchers, or magazines, any reduction in staying power also incurs a proportional reduction in combat power. So we assume that 50 percent damage not only means that staying power is reduced by half, but it also means that the ability to apply offensive and defensive combat power is reduced by half. The transition from equation 1.4 to equation 1.5 shows how this approach to proportional damage assessment is applied in the calculations.

Since the analysis is not meant to be predictive, analysts need to keep in mind the artificiality of proportionally attributing damage. In actual combat, a single missile hit on a ship with a staying power of two hits could very likely disable all the ship's combat power, yet the hull could steam on; alternatively the single hit could render the ship dead in the water, but the ship could retain full fighting strength. Exactly where a missile hits a ship's hull or superstructure determines what specific damage is incurred, but since substantial destructive power is delivered with each salvo weapon, a relatively small number of hits can put quite a large ship out of action. Therefore, once multiple hits have been absorbed by a ship, the results of comparative and predictive analysis converge.

1.5 SALVO WARFARE WITH UNMANNED SYSTEMS

Unmanned systems offer an unprecedented opportunity to once again change the character of naval warfare. In the very near future (and to a modest extent already today), ships will be able to package their combat power into autonomous off-board vehicles. We already see how sensors have literally taken flight in UAVs; soon antiship missiles and antimissile missiles will be air-, surface- and perhaps even subsurface-deployable by similar means. The U.S. Navy has demonstrated how cooperative engagement capability can allow one ship to control another ship's air defense missiles, and the Navy routinely practices UAV handoffs between platforms. We should expect that advances in these capabilities that will allow a wider range of ship–vehicle interactions, more handoffs between platforms, and a broader reconfiguration of combat power among a force. In short, vehicle autonomy will improve, and as it does vehicles will become more independent of their home platforms (perhaps to the point that the notion of a "home platform" becomes obsolete).

Let's look at another kind of sequential salvo exchange to explore how distributing combat power in this way can be a leverage point in modern combat. Assume two three-ship task groups as before, side A and side B. These ships have the following characteristics: $\alpha = \beta = 4$, $a_1 = b_1 = 2$ and $a_3 = b_3 = 3$. Side A, however, is able to distribute its offensive and defensive combat power among off-board autonomous vehicles, and the hull retains only sustainment and command and control functions. Side A is therefore not susceptible to proportional damage, yet side B is configured in the usual way. After the first salvo,

$$\frac{\Delta B}{B} = \frac{4(3) - 3(3)}{2(3)} = \frac{12 - 9}{6} = 0.50,$$

$$\frac{\Delta A}{A} = \frac{4(3) - 3(3)}{2(3)} = \frac{12 - 9}{6} = 0.50.$$

Side B loses a ship and a half (of proportional damage). Side A's combat power is not reduced when its staying power is reduced by half, so side A's one and a half ships now can fight like three (except, of course, for staying power).[2] In the second salvo,

$$\frac{\Delta B}{B} = \frac{4(3) - 3(1.5)}{2(1.5)} = \frac{12 - 4.5}{3} = 2.50,$$

$$\frac{\Delta A}{A} = \frac{4(1.5) - 3(3)}{2(1.5)} = \frac{6 - 9}{3} = -1.00.$$

Side A receives no further damage while side B is annihilated.

1.6 THE SALVO EXCHANGE SET AND COMBAT ENTROPY

Significant inefficiencies can exist in salvo exchanges. To better understand the source and effects of salvo inefficiencies, it is necessary to look at the set of outcomes for individual salvos in greater detail. As will be seen, the salvo equations are an optimistic theoretical upper bound for the outcome of a salvo. Two concepts, the salvo exchange set and combat entropy, show how things can be much worse for the combatants (and much, *much* worse for side B during the salvo exchanges in section 1.3).

The salvo exchange set describes the different possible outcomes of salvo exchanges. It is defined as

$$S \equiv \{(H \cap D) \cup (H \cap D') \cup (H' \cap D) \cup (H' \cap D')\} \tag{1.4}$$

where **H** is the event that offense weapons are properly targeted and will hit their intended targets and **D** is the event that the defense is successful in destroying inbound weapons.[3]

Until weapons are used, they have combat potential, which in a perfectly efficient system should equal the damage inflicted by their use. If salvo exchanges were perfectly efficient, the only member in the salvo exchange set would be **(H ∩ D)**. Since examples of the other three subsets abound, the system is clearly not perfectly efficient. This loss of efficiency is called combat entropy. The four subsets resulting from the salvo exchange set are defined below. A brief discussion of each subset's contribution to combat entropy is included.

Subset 1. **H ∩ D: The defense counters correctly targeted shots.**

This is the most efficient case.[4]

Subset 2. **H ∩ D': The defense does not counter correctly targeted shots.**

Combat power is wasted by the unsuccessful expense of counterfire. Still worse, unsuccessful "double-teaming" may occur.

Subset 3. **H' ∩ D: The defense counters incorrectly targeted shots.**

Combat power is lost by ineffective offensive targeting and by expense of counterfire on a nonthreat. Still worse, unnecessary double-teaming may occur.

Subset 4. **H' ∩ D': The defense does not counter incorrectly targeted shots.**

Here combat power is lost by ineffective offensive targeting and ineffective counterfire. Aside from simple misses, two effects, the "weapon-sump effect" (some targets are hit by more than their share of weapons while others do not receive enough hits) and "overkill" (the assignment of more weapons to all targets than are required) are often operative in this case.

The combat entropy defined above is a result of the physics of salvo exchanges, e.g., radar inaccuracies or ineffective distribution of combat power. The sheer randomness of salvo exchanges also causes combat entropy. Even a "simple" scenario in which three units of side B each fire four missiles at one unit of side A will result in 4^{12} (almost 17 million) possible outcomes. Experiments have shown that as much as 30 percent of combat potential can be lost to entropy in this "simple" exchange.

Combat entropy increases as the numbers of shooters and targets increase. Reexamining the salvo exchanges in section 1.3 from this perspective, we see that side B's targeting challenge is much more complex than side A's. While side A need only consider the complications of distributing offensive combat power among three targets, Side B could be shooting at as many as twenty-one: three hulls (to be hit twice each), twelve off-board vehicles each carrying one offensive missile, and six off-board vehicles each carrying one defensive missile. The combinatorics mean, of course, that side B's targeting and coordination problem is not seven times worse but many, many orders of magnitude more complicated, an additional leverage point that makes distributing combat power even more beneficial for side A.

1.7 TACTICAL CONSIDERATIONS

Given that side B now has twenty-one targets to consider (and perhaps another fifteen or so after the first salvo if side B attacks off-board vehicles in addition to hulls), side B's β values would have to carry an unusually large complement of antiship missiles. Alternatively, side B's navy could invest in smaller ordnance, specially designed to combat smaller off-board vehicles. Assuming side B can overcome the daunting search and targeting challenges of twenty-one simultaneous engagements, it is instructive to see how distribution and reconfiguration allow side A to employ a variety of tactical adaptations, yet another leverage point for forces that can achieve a high level of independence with their unmanned vehicles.

The baseline tactical case is outlined in section 1.3. Side B attacks side A using traditional antiship missiles targeted at the hulls. As we have seen, side A can rely on handoffs and reconfiguration to overcome side B by the second salvo. What if side B focuses its efforts on attacking the unmanned vehicles with smaller missiles? In this case, side A is wise to disperse into three separate groups so that side B can find only one-third of the targets at once. Even if this third is lost, side A will still have two-thirds of its force free to fire at side B, which will now have its position established by the located one-third of side A. All of side A missiles can now attack faster than side B can find the rest of the missing adversary force.

What if side B, frustrated in its efforts to focus on first hulls and then off-board vehicles, develops a capability to electronically jam side A's control frequencies (or links)? In this case side A might mass its hulls to control its off-board platforms using shorter range directed links, similar to jam-resistant line-of-sight links used by shipboard helicopters today. Further frustrated in this nonkinetic attempt, side B would be relegated to again attacking hulls or vehicles and all the challenges of managing offensive fires against twenty-one targets.

One aspect of salvo warfare not addressed in equation 1.1, but covered in other versions of the salvo equations, is scouting effectiveness, the ability to find and fix the enemy for effective offensive shots. While even legacy warships have off-board vehicles for search (the most prominent being the ship-based helicopter), proportional damage will work much the same way with scouting effectiveness on these platforms as it does with offensive and defensive combat power. Some "cross-decking" of helicopters is possible, but shipboard flight-deck space is very limited. In addition, radars and sensors attached to the superstructure will be damaged when the ship is hit. Conversely, a force that can distribute or reconfigure search assets will have a decided advantage in targeting a second salvo, yet another leverage point for unmanned vehicles in modern naval combat.

1.8 CONCLUSION

This appendix has presented a theoretical basis for analyzing warfare between a legacy force and a force with a large number of independent, unmanned off-board vehicles. It has shown how the salvo equations can be used to identify tactical advantages for forces with unmanned systems as well as the vulnerabilities inherent in the way forces are constituted today. The introduction suggested that this approach could deliver a revolutionary change in warfighting capability for the LCS program, among others. For this result to occur, of course, requires advances in autonomy, networking, and control that are not yet realized as well as a fundamental shift in thinking—and investment—among senior naval leaders.

In some ways, however, this appendix has set up a false argument. If the U.S. Navy has such a fundamental shift in thinking and investment, then others will follow suit, and the LCS's problem will not be a fight against a legacy force but a fight against an adversary much more like itself. No one yet knows exactly how a distributed, networked force will fight a distributed, networked force, although some formulations have been attempted.[5] The United States is not the only nation pursuing advanced autonomy, networking, and control, so it is not guaranteed to be the world leader in developing these capabilities. If it fails to do so, as it has already with LCS, then it will be quite ironic indeed when LCS cannot fight in either of the worlds of legacy or future naval combat.

REFERENCES

Jeffrey R. Cares, "The Fundamentals of Salvo Warfare," pp. 31–41, Naval Postgraduate School masters' thesis, Monterey, Calif., 1990.

Wayne P. Hughes Jr., "A Salvo Model of Warships in Missile Combat Used to Evaluate Their Staying Power," *Naval Research Logistics* 42 (1995): 267–89.

NOTES

INTRODUCTION

Epigraph: J. C. Wylie, "On Maritime Strategy," U.S. Naval Institute *Proceedings* 79, no. 5 (May 1953): 467–77.

1. For a treatise on how war at sea differs from war on land, see Julian S. Corbett, *Some Principles of Maritime Strategy* (London: Longmans, Green, 1911), 155–61.

2. Bradley A. Fiske, "American Naval Policy," U.S. Naval Institute *Proceedings* 31, no. 1/113 (January 1905), https://www.usni.org/maga zines/proceedings/1905-01/american-naval-policy. If the reader feels that the authors, while achieving only captain's rank, presume too much to write about what admirals should or shouldn't know, consider that Fiske penned these words as a "mere" commander.

3. If available, the Naval Institute Press' 1988 revised edition in the Classics of Sea Power series is recommended to the reader, so as to benefit from Wayne Hughes' helpful introduction, context, and comments.

4. Fiske, "American Naval Policy."

5. J. C. Wylie, "Why a Sailor Thinks Like a Sailor," U.S. Naval Institute *Proceedings* 83, no. 8/654 (August 1957), https://www.usni.org/maga zines/proceedings/1957-08/why-sailor-thinks-sailor.

6. Again, the Classics of Sea Power 1989 version is recommended, in this case to benefit from Naval War College professor John Hattendorf's guidance.

7. These briefings can be found at the Air Power Australia website, http://www.ausairpower.net/APA-Boyd-Papers.html, accessed 27 October 2020.

8. The third edition of *Fleet Tactics* is now in print. Wayne P. Hughes Jr. and Robert Girrier, *Fleet Tactics and Naval Operations*, 3rd ed. (Annapolis, Md.: Naval Institute Press, 2018).

9. Command, control, communications, computers, intelligence, surveillance, and reconnaissance.

CHAPTER 1. NAVAL POWER

1. A discussion of how naval power is applied against air and ground power in joint operations, while important to the modern reader, is beyond the scope of this chapter.

2. Even advanced hull shapes that slice through water differently can't go too much faster than conventional hulls without extreme fuel penalties.

3. For example, a common merchant container ship load is about 5,000 twenty-foot equivalent units (TEUs—the standard shipping container). TEUs average about 12 tons each.

4. Which is why, as Wayne Hughes notes in Fiske's text, we man a navy but equip an army.

5. Who has defined the companion skill to "generalship" and "admiralship" for a numbered air force?

6. To grasp the magnitude of the army's sustainment challenge, consider that a World War II division required about one Liberty ship worth of supplies per week (about the same tonnage as in the buoyancy example, above), so a numbered army on the move might require eight to ten such loads received and staged at a friendly port each week for perhaps a month, and then delivered along increasingly long lines of communication.

7. This example is provided not to argue that navies are better than air or ground forces but simply to explain how and why fleets are very different in the way their military power is constituted, transported, and applied.

8. Not to mention the "prize" value to the captain and crew. Moreover, manpower could be cheaper than cannon and hulls in the age of sail.

9. While aircraft, the submarine, and self-propelled torpedoes grew in importance from the start of the twentieth century onward, gunnery retained its prominence during this period.

10. On civilian industry, see, for example, Frederick Winslow Taylor, in his 1911 book *Principles of Scientific Management* (New York: Harper, 1911).

11. Chase's 1902 paper remained classified until 1972, so his equations are eponymous to F. W. Lanchester, who developed them thirteen years later than Chase (and one year later than M. Osipov, a Russian). For the full story about the development of these equations, see Bradley A. Fiske, *The Navy as a Fighting Machine* (1917), rev. ed., ed. Wayne P. Hughes (Annapolis, Md.: Naval Institute Press, 1988), appendix C. An abbreviated account is in appendix B of this text.

12. World War II saw the introduction of guided missiles in naval warfare, but their use was limited. Kamikaze airplanes, very much like guided missiles, saw extensive use in the Pacific, to devastating pulse-power effect.

13. Staying power is not necessarily the amount of combat power required to actually sink the hull of a ship. There are other types of "kills" in naval combat, such as "mission kills" (ship unable to fight but still afloat) or "mobility kills" (ship able to fight but not move).

14. For simplicity here, the ships on a side are assumed to be identical to each other. See appendix A of this volume for Hughes' most comprehensive treatment of salvo warfare mathematics.

15. The symbol ∩ denotes "and," the symbol ∪ denotes "or," and X′ denotes the complement of X.

16. To read values from such a chart, think of this as its geographical equivalent, a map of a hill. Say that a climber starts at point (1.0, 1.0) and starts climbing upward (toward the crest) at (0.5, 0.5) the point of maximum entropy. The climber would pass the first "altitude" gradient of 0.1 at (0.97, 0.97). At about (0.95, 0.95), the climber would be about halfway between gradient 0.1 and 0.2, or at an entropy value of about 0.15. The gradients get farther apart as the climber approaches higher gradients, indicating a sharp initial climb followed by smoother grade toward the maximum.

17. See appendix A for a full embellishment of the salvo equations, including softkill defenses.

18. Thomas R. Beall, "The Development of a Naval Battle Model and Its Validation Using Historical Data," master's thesis (U.S. Naval Postgraduate School, Monterey, Calif., 1990).

19. John C. Schulte, "An Analysis of the Historical Effectiveness of Anti-Ship Cruise Missiles in Littoral Warfare," paper, U.S. Naval Postgraduate School, Monterey, Calif., 1994.

20. Although a full-throated critique of the state of naval analysis as practiced in places like the Pentagon is beyond the scope of this book, the fact that so few books such as this one exist is evidence of either broad consensus and agreement on the topic or of benign neglect (the reader's opinion of which one it is likely depends on where they are employed).

21. This is an artifact of Cold War realism: designers assumed that no ship would withstand a tactical nuclear hit at sea, so armor seemed useless and was no longer considered a critical ship design feature. For their part, Navy budgeteers were happy not to pay for the extra fuel required to propel hundreds of ships with hundreds of tons of extra weight over their thirty- to forty-year service lives. Fleet commanders, who value a ship's *combat life* over its service life, are to this day ill-served by this decision.

22. Joseph Bolmarchic, "Who Shoots How Many?", unpublished briefing slides, Quantics Incorporated © 2000, 2003, 2010.

23. The triangles in the figure are the actual cumulative data points scaled so that the axes both read as percentages (a double cumulative presentation). The curve is the multivariate Polya distribution that fits the data. For a full description of the method, see Jeffrey R. Cares, "An Exploration of Performance Distributions in Collectives," in *Operations Research for Unmanned Systems*, Cares and Dickmann (Hoboken, N.J.: Wiley, 2016).

24. "Command Summary of Fleet Admiral Chester W. Nimitz, USN: Volume 1 of 8; Running Estimate and Summary Maintained by Captain James M Steele, USN, CINCPAC Staff at Pearl Harbor, Hawaii, Covering the Period 7 December 1941 to 31 August 1942," U.S. Naval War College, Naval Historical Collection Archives, Box 58, Folder 5, RG-24, https://usnwcarchives.org/repositories/2/archival_objects/29382.

25. Department of the Navy, *Navy Planning*, NWP 5-01, December 2013, http://dnnlgwick.blob.core.windows.net/portals/10/MAWS/5-01 _(Dec_2013)_(NWP)-(Promulgated).pdf?sr=b&si=DNNFileMan agerPolicy&sig=un5q%2FWUW21Qzq52MmQ7KMfD%2FhHM dj%2Frp1xJSur5TF58%3D (29 Oct 2020). The relative combat power analysis process is found in appendix E.

CHAPTER 2. SEARCH AND SURVEILLANCE

1. This first rendition of this matrix was developed by Dr. John T. Hanley Jr. while he was deputy director of the Chief of Naval Operations Strategic Studies Group.
2. Negative information is what a detector might infer about a target when there is no detection.
3. A false detection occurs when a detection system detects a target when none is present. A failed detection occurs when a detection system does not detect a target when one is present.
4. The random search algorithm is derived in Bernard Osgood Koopman, *Search and Screening*, OEG Report No. 56 (Washington, D.C.: Office of the Chief of Naval Operations, 1946), https://www.informs.org /Explore/History-of-O.R.-Excellence/Documents/Bernard-O.-Koop man-Search-and-Screening-1946. While the mathematics is not too difficult, it is involved enough not to include here.
5. We can think of a worse search, perhaps an "ignorant search algorithm," in which the searcher avoids detecting the target. Such "searches" would more properly be part of "hider theory."
6. The binomial probability law is:
$$P(X = k) = \frac{n!}{k!(n-k)!} \, p^k(1-p)^{n-k}$$
   where n, k are integers and $n \geq k$; and $0 < p < 1$.
7. The choice of the same search area is useful for this comparison, but one common mistake made by search planners is that, by determining a search area, they somehow compel the target to contain itself within that area. Of course, the target chooses where the target goes, not the searcher.

CHAPTER 3. LOGISTICS AND MANEUVER

1. For example, a mechanized division requires fuel and food for more than 3,000 vehicles and 20,000 personnel. A field army might be at least triple this size.

2. Before the cause of scurvy was identified in 1747, a ship needed fresh food at least every ninety days. Even after scurvy was cured, however, a ship couldn't go much longer than that without morale and crew performance suffering from a poor diet.

3. Near misses often caused so much damage in World War II naval combat that many referred to them as being more like "near hits."

4. Chapter 5 addresses how these considerations might be different in the Robotics Age.

5. Ensuring this happens at the right place and at the right time with the right predominance of combat power (and enough information about the enemy to properly apply it) is the most difficult act in naval operations; this is fully explored in the next chapter.

6. The reader can calculate exactly how much coverage the surge force can achieve by locating lead time (in days) on the horizontal axis of figure 2.6 and reading the percent coverage where lead time crosses the perfect sweep and random sweep curves.

7. Recall from the earlier discussion that maneuvers during approach and attack use more speed, which depletes fuel stores much more quickly than during efficient cruising.

8. For a discussion of aspects of this issue, see Anthony Cowden, "Expeditionary or Forward Based?," *RealClearDefense*, July 23, 2019, https://www.realcleardefense.com/articles/2019/07/23/expeditionary _or_forward_based_114601.html.

CHAPTER 4. CONTROL

1. J. C. Wylie, "On Maritime Strategy," U.S. Naval Institute *Proceedings* 79, no. 5 (May 1953): 467–77.

2. Although modern literature uses the term "blockade" as interdiction of both military and commercial vessels, we revert to the classic definitions of "blockade" for military vessels in the vicinity of its harbors and "quarantine" for commercial traffic in the same areas. "Commerce raiding" defines cargo destruction or seizure on the open seas. Blockades

(and quarantines) can be both close (near harbors) or distant (away from harbors but nonetheless directed at traffic flowing to or from them).

3. Of course, a blockading force also quarantines the same port, leading to the axiom to "make the enemy's coast your frontier."

4. As a perennial inferior fleet relative to the Royal Navy, French policy on submarine development was aptly summed up by Adm. Edmond Jurien de la Gravière in 1885: "Everything which threatens *les colosses* (the giants) and tends to emancipate *les moucherons* (the gnats) should be warmly welcomed by the French Navy." Quoted in Bernard Brodie, *Sea Power in the Machine Age* (Princeton, N.J.: Princeton University Press, 1941) 287.

5. The "modern" concept of anti-access/area denial (A2/AD) is in fact more than 150 years old. It was discussed at length by Fiske and Corbett, seemingly forgotten, and then reinvented at the end of the Cold War.

6. Or, to be consistent, commerce raider.

7. Interestingly, this twenty-five or so to one ratio of hunter to hunted persists to this day. Submarine warfare is indeed an effective cost-imposing investment strategy.

8. This was especially true of the Imperial Japanese Navy, who were entirely Mahanian in their thinking.

9. Naval War College Archives, Records of the Course of Advanced Study: President, Naval War College, letter to the Chief of Naval Operations, A3-1 serial 2354-51, 1 May 1951. Cited in J. C. Wylie, *Military Strategy: A General Theory of Power Control* (Annapolis, Md.: Naval Institute Press, 1989), xxii.

10. Wylie, *Military Strategy*, 22–23.

11. Wylie, 23.

12. First printed in 1943, von Neumann and Oskar Morgenstern's *Theory of Games and Economic Behavior* introduced the formal study of games to economists, psychologists, and business and military strategists. The calculus of Cold War nuclear deterrence, for example, was heavily influenced by game theory.

13. Lest the reader think tic-tac-toe is too simple of an example, consider that there are 255,168 unique games that can be played, 131,184 won by the first player, 77,904 won by the second player and 46,080 drawn. The patterns are highly repetitive, however, resulting in only a few

opening gambits, each of which leads the players down very predictable paths. See Jesper Juul, "255,168 Ways of Playing Tic Tac Toe," *The Ludologist*, 28 December 2003, https://www.jesperjuul.net/ludologist/2003/12/28/255168-ways-of-playing-tic-tac-toe/. How more complicated is this than the common Joint planning practice of selecting three friendly and three enemy courses of action and then building a tree of branches and sequels?

14. For a discussion and analysis of the complexity of the seven phases of the Battle of the Atlantic, see Charles M. Sternhell and Alan M. Thorndike, *Antisubmarine Warfare in World War II*, OEG Report 51 (Washington, D.C.: Office of the Chief of Naval Operations, 1946), http://www.ibiblio.org/hyperwar/USN/rep/ASW-51/.

15. Wylie, *Military Strategy*, 71–72.

16. But also quite reluctantly, in part because many thought joint language couldn't adequately capture the essence of naval operations. It is worth noting that Wylie's original motives were similar, and his products might have been the exact ammunition needed to push back against the current one-size-fits-all joint doctrine.

17. This situation is starting to be rectified with a recent reemphasis on the "navalization" of the Naval War College.

18. Moreover, A2/AD forces are not built to project to our shores.

19. It was the same B. O. Koopman of search theory fame who came up with the formulation that two forces of size m and n, respectively, can interact in as many as 2^{2mn} different ways, in his excellent 1970 report, "A Study of the Logical Basis of Combat Simulation," *Operations Research* 18, no. 5: 855–82.

20. See appendix C.

21. Cyber warfare has for too long focused exclusively on IT-related aspects of competition. True cyber warfare employs and exploits all three domains of competition.

CHAPTER 5. FIGHTING FLEETS IN THE ROBOTIC AGE

1. Jeffrey R. Cares, "Distributed Combat Power: The Application of Salvo Theory to Unmanned Systems," in *Operations Research for Unmanned Systems*, ed. Jeffrey R. Cares and John Q. Dickmann Jr., 287–94 (New York: Wiley, 2016).

2. This vignette was first presented in preparation for a wargame series at the CNO Strategic Studies Group in 1998. See Jeffrey R. Cares, "Adaptive Forces," Presentation to the Complexity Working Group, Newport, R.I., 4 March 1999.

APPENDIX A. SALVO MODEL OF WARSHIPS IN MISSILE COMBAT USED TO EVALUATE THEIR STAYING POWER

1. Originally published in *Naval Research Logistics* 42 (1995): 267–89, © John Wiley & Sons, Inc. This article is a U.S. government work and as such is in the public domain in the United States of America.
2. Originally "bold and centered" read "underlined." Change made to reflect format changes for publishing in this volume.

APPENDIX B. THE SALVO EQUATIONS AND FORCE PLANNING

1. Department of the Navy, Chief of Naval Operations, *Navy Planning NWP 5-01*, December 2013, http://dnnlgwick.blob.core.windows.net/portals/10/MAWS/5-01_(Dec_2013)_(NWP)-(Promulgated).pdf?sr=b&si=DNNFileManagerPolicy&sig=un5q%2FWUW21Qzq52M mQ7KMfD%2FhHMdj%2Frp1xJSur5TF58%3D. The RCPA process is found in annex E.
2. While this procedure is a two-sided force-on-force example, it is also—when suitably modified—valid for one-sided use in planning joint theater air and missile defense schemes for protecting defended asset list targets or fleet air defense against land-based salvos.
3. Some sophistication can be achieved by biasing the width of intervals to account for, say, a higher radar cross-section for a particular ship class than the others in a formation.
4. Note that since side A has the larger salvo size that leakers for side B grow disproportionally relative to those of side A as the leaker rate is increased.
5. Note that D_A is a smooth curve from 0 percent to 30 percent leakage, while D_B shows more of an advantage for side B at 0 percent and 20 percent than at 10 percent leakage. This is due to the integer effects of rounding error in the leakage calculations. Allowing an extra half a missile to leak at the 20 percent level would, on average, bring D_B up to 88 percent, but rounding up to eleven leakers would have produced too

much damage. This underscores the conditional that when both sides are close to parity, there can be a significant difference in the outcome of a battle when even one more or one less missile impacts a force.

6. Planners should look at a range of leakage rates. Only two are presented here for exposition and brevity.

APPENDIX C. DECONSTRUCTING C4ISR

1. The naval operational architecture (NOA) is the latest proposal to build such a system, as FORCEnet and NCW were before it.
2. At its core, tactics is the sequencing and arrangement of combat assets in time and space. Our modern word "tactics" comes directly from the Greek *taktos*, meaning "the order or arrangement of things."
3. For a complete discussion of information conditions, scale, and the modern C4ISR model, see Jeffrey R. Cares, *Distributed Networked Operations: The Foundations of Network Centric Warfare* (Newport, R.I.: Alidade Press, 2006).
4. See Department of the Army, *Mission Command*, US Army Doctrine Publication (ADP) 6-0, (Washington, D.C.: Department of the Army, 17 May 2014).
5. The Aegis Combat System is the epitome of a well-engineered, well-interpreted system of connected computers, even when scaled up to multiship operations.

APPENDIX D. DISTRIBUTED COMBAT POWER

1. Jeffrey R. Cares, "Distributed Combat Power: The Application of Salvo Theory to Unmanned Systems," in *Operations Research for Unmanned Vehicles*, ed. Jeffrey R. Cares and John Q. Dickmann Jr. (New York: Wiley, 2016), 287–94.
2. This assumes a modest magazine or a reload capability on the unmanned platforms, perhaps up to the original α and a_3 values.
3. X' denotes the complement of X, that is, "not X."
4. Some combat power may be wasted if the defense has an unequal distribution of counterfire and "double teams" inbound weapons.
5. See, for example, Jeffrey R. Cares, *Distributed Networked Operations: The Foundations of Network Centric Warfare* (Newport, R.I.: Alidade Press, 2006).

BIBLIOGRAPHY

Beall, Thomas R. "The Development of a Naval Battle Model and Its Validation Using Historical Data." Master's thesis. Naval Postgraduate School, Monterey, Calif., 1990.

Bolmarchic, Joseph. "Who Shoots How Many?" Unpublished briefing slides, Quantics Incorporated © 2000, 2003, 2010.

Brodie, Bernard. *Sea Power in the Machine Age.* Princeton, N.J.: Princeton University Press, 1941.

Cares, Jeffrey R. "Adaptive Forces." Presentation to the Complexity Working Group, Newport, R.I., 4 March 1999.

———. "Distributed Combat Power: The Application of Salvo Theory to Unmanned Systems." In *Operations Research for Unmanned Systems*, ed. Jeffrey R. Cares and John Q. Dickmann Jr., 287–94. New York: John Wiley, 2016.

———. *Distributed Networked Operations: The Foundations of Network Centric Warfare.* Newport, R.I.: Alidade Press, 2006.

———. "An Exploration of Performance Distributions in Collectives." In *Operations Research for Unmanned Systems*, ed. Jeffrey R. Cares and John Q. Dickmann Jr., 271–86. New York: John Wiley, 2016.

———. "The Fundamentals of Salvo Warfare." Master's thesis, Naval Postgraduate School, Monterey, Calif., 1990.

Corbett, Julian S. *Some Principles of Maritime Strategy.* London: Longmans, Green, 1911.

Cowden, Anthony. "Expeditionary or Forward Based?" *RealClearDefense*, July 23, 2019. https://www.realcleardefense.com/articles/2019/07/23/expeditionary_or_forward_based_114601.html.

Department of the Army. *Mission Command*, US Army Doctrine Publication (ADP) 6-0. Washington, D.C.: Department of the Army, 17 May 2014.

Fiske, Bradley A. "American Naval Policy." U.S. Naval Institute *Proceedings* 31, no. 1/113 (January 1905). https://www.usni.org/magazines/proceedings/1905-01/american-naval-policy.

———. *The Navy as a Fighting Machine* (1917), rev. ed., ed. Wayne P. Hughes. Annapolis, Md.: Naval Institute Press, 1988.

Hughes, Wayne P., Jr. "A Salvo Model of Warships in Missile Combat Used to Evaluate Their Staying Power." *Naval Research Logistics* 42 (1995): 267–89.

Hughes, Wayne P., Jr., and Robert Girrier. *Fleet Tactics and Naval Operations*, 3rd ed. Annapolis, Md.: Naval Institute Press, 2018.

Koopman, Bernard Osgood. *Search and Screening*, OEG Report No. 56. Washington, D.C.: Office of the Chief of Naval Operations, 1946. https://www.informs.org/Explore/History-of-O.R.-Excellence/Documents/Bernard-O.-Koopman-Search-and-Screening-1946.

———. "A Study of the Logical Basis of Combat Simulation." *Operations Research* 18, no. 5: 855–82.

McCue, Brian. *U-Boats in the Bay of Biscay: An Essay in Operations Analysis*. Newport, R.I.: Alidade Press, 2008.

Schulte, John C. "An Analysis of the Historical Effectiveness of Anti-Ship Cruise Missiles in Littoral Warfare." Paper, Naval Postgraduate School, Monterey, Calif., 1994.

Speller, Ian. *Understanding Naval Warfare*. London: Routledge, 2014.

Sternhell, Charles M., and Alan M. Thorndike. *Antisubmarine Warfare in World War II*, OEG Report 51. Washington, D.C.: Office of the Chief of Naval Operations, 1946. http://www.ibiblio.org/hyperwar/USN/rep/ASW-51/.

Tangredi, Sam J. *Anti-Access Warfare: Countering A2/AD Strategies*. Annapolis, Md.: Naval Institute Press, 2013.

Taylor, Frederick Winslow. *Principles of Scientific Management*. New York: Harper, 1911.

Wylie, J. C. *Military Strategy: A General Theory of Power Control* (1967); rev. ed., ed. John Hattendorf. Classics of Sea Power series. 1989; repr. Annapolis, Md.: Naval Institute Press, 2014.

———. "Why a Sailor Thinks Like a Sailor." U.S. Naval Institute *Proceedings* 83, no. 8/654 (August 1957). https://www.usni.org/magazines/proceedings/1957-08/why-sailor-thinks-sailor.

INDEX

accuracy of fire, definition, 122
accurate shots: definition, 122; fighting
  power and, 123; scouting effectiveness and, 124
Ace Factor, 25–27
acquisition process: preoccupation with,
  3. *See also* procurement studies
active defense system, 22
active surveillance systems, 33
adaptive planning. *See* uncertainty, planning for
admiralship: Fiske on, 4, 13. *See also*
  operational art
adversary uncertainty: molecule-bit-staff
  model of information and, 78–79;
  planning for, 68, 75–77; reason to
  profit from combat and, 79. *See also*
  area of uncertainty; uncertainty, planning for
Aegis Combat System, 24, 119, 172n5
  (Appendix C)
aggregation: concentrating for combat,
  hourglass pattern and, 54–55, 76–77,
  81, 168n5; naval power in Robotics
  Age and, 86
Air Force, U.S.: Ace Factor and, 25–27;
  aviation communications on control,
  147; fuel for airfreight carriers of,
  12–13
air power (aircraft): comparing naval
  power with, 14, 164n5; detection
  methods against, 32; in multistage
  systems, 82–84; in Red–Blue vignette,

88–90, 91; surveillance of irregularities by, 43; Wylie on force-strategy
  combinations for, 66. *See also*
  unmanned air vehicles
air traffic, neutral, false or invaluable
  targets and, 42
airborne combat direction center
  (ABCDC), Blue assets controlled by,
  90–91, 92, 93
aircraft carriers, 82–83, 107, 119
airfreight carriers (C-5), 12–13
all weather forces, 31
"American Naval Policy" (Fiske), 4, 6,
  163nn2–3
Ancker, C. J., Jr., 133
anti-access/area denial (A2/AD), 72,
  169n5, 170n18
antisubmarine warfare (ASW), 64
approach: fuel requirements for, 57,
  168n7; as naval maneuver skill, 52,
  53, 59; transition to attack formation
  from, 54
Arab–Israeli War (1973), 24
area defense missiles, point defense systems compared with, 138
area of uncertainty (AOU): insufficient
  for engagement, 44; measuring the
  common operational picture and,
  39–41; search within, 33
armor: for nuclear hit, fuel and, 166n21;
  staying power and, 25, 104–5
army: dependence on logistics, 14,
  164n6; fuel and food requirements,

fighting power: Chase's equation of continuous fire article on, 130–31, 132; definition, 123; equations for, 115

fighting strength: definition, 123–24; hits and, 121; salvo equations for, 111

fire (fires, firing): first, effectively, 28, 119; separate from maneuver for ground and joint operations, 57–58. *See also* continuous fire; pulse combat

firepower: definition, 122–23; fighting strength and, 123; in ground combat, 133; hits and, 121

first move, taking third move as, 80

Fiske, Bradley: "American Naval Policy," 4, 163nn2–3; on anti-access/area denial, 169n5; on basic fleet functions, 79; on expecting genius on demand, 101; naval operational art and, 8; on naval power and ground power, 14; on naval power as mechanical power, 13; *The Navy as a Fighting Machine*, 5–6; on power, 11; principles of naval warfare and, 98; wisdom of, xiii, 71

flag officers: control lessons for, 79–81; heuristics of centralized computers and, 151; logistics and maneuver lessons for, 58–59; naval operational art and, 4; salvo warfare lessons for, 27–29; search and surveillance lessons for, 45–47; as veterans of demanding at-sea combat problems, 101

flanking, of screening forces, 73, 75

fleet planners (fleet plans): campaign design using fleet functions by, 75–76; control lessons for, 79–81; heuristics of centralized computers and, 151; leakage analysis, 171–72nn4–6; logistics and maneuver lessons for, 58–59; salvo equations and, 137–43, 171n2 (Appendix B); salvo warfare lessons for, 27–29; search and surveillance lessons for, 45–47; wargaming and, 100

Fleet Tactics (Hughes), 7, 28, 97

fleet-in-being, definition, 62

fleets: action in Missile Age, 23–25; detection environment and targets for, 31–32; distributed combat and, 86–87; fleet-on-fleet competitions, 100–101; functions of, 8, 71–73, 170n19; games to learn how to win for, 100; inferior, fleet-in-being as, 62; naval operational art heritage

and, 5; Nimitz on principles of war and, 97–98; oceanic information conditions and, 74–75; operational art language for, 3; planning, salvo equations and, 9; prime objective of, 61. *See also* combat power; hourglass pattern; maneuver

force: concentration of, maneuver and, 54–55, 168n5; sufficiency, salvo equations as measures of, 18, 156–57. *See also* combat power

force strength, definition, 121

FORCEnet, 172n1

force-on-force equations: differential, in Chase's article, 130; embellishment of, 115–16; for pulse combat, 16–19; by a single salvo, 110. *See also* salvo equations

four-element salvo model, in force-on-force analysis, 129

fractional exchange ratio (FER): to compare equal-cost configurations of naval forces, 103; definition, 127; enemy attributes and, 118; as measure of effectiveness, 110, 111–12; salvo equations as measures of, 18, 112–13, 156–57

fuel: armor for nuclear hit and, 166n21; daily requirements, 49–50; efficiency, hull size and, 12–13, 164nn2–3; operational maneuver and, 168n7. *See also* refueling

game theory: Cold War nuclear deterrence and, 169n12; as deadly, human cost of, 81; on information conditions of competition, 74; von Neumann and, 66–67; Wylie on war planning and, 67–68. *See also* non–strictly determined games; strictly determined games; uncertainty, planning for

Georgia, Russia's conflict with, xii

Germany, Battle of Jutland and, 129

Gibbs Entropy (*S*), 20–21. *See also* combat entropy

goats: Ace Factor and, 26–27; human performance and, 29

Golden Age of Tactical Thought (ca. 1880–1914), 5–6, 98. *See also* New Golden Age

Goldwater–Nichols Act (1986), 3, 69, 98. *See also* jointness

ABOUT THE AUTHORS

Jeffrey R. Cares is the CEO of Alidade Incorporated and a retired U.S. Navy captain. As a thought-leader in Information Age military innovation, he consults at the most senior levels of the international defense industry and lectures internationally and at service colleges on the future of combat. He is the author of *Distributed Networked Operations: The Foundations of Network Centric Warfare* and *Operations Research for Unmanned Systems*, in addition to pioneering work in the application of complex systems research to military problems.

Anthony Cowden attended the University of Michigan under the Naval Reserve Officers Training Corps (NROTC), where he received his BA in history. He received his MS degree in computer science from the University of New Haven and his MA degree in national security and strategic studies from the U.S. Naval War College. After nearly five years on active duty, Cowden joined Sonalysts, Inc., and affiliated with the Navy Reserve. After a twenty-year Reserve career Captain Cowden returned to active duty in 2009 and retired after thirty-seven years as a commissioned officer in 2021.

.